# FIRE IN THE ISLANDS!

## ALISON GRIFFITHS

The Acts of the Holy Spirit in the Solomons

Harold Shaw Publishers
Wheaton, Illinois

*cover photo: Ronald Griffiths*

*Copyright © 1977 by*
*Harold Shaw Publishers*




*ISBN 0-87788-264-9*
*Library of Congress Catalog Card Number 77-71627*

*Printed in the United States of America*

# Table of Contents

# Foreword

*This book tells a story, but the story is a true one. The narrative is closely based on the historical record. For example, Florence Young's thoughts and opinions as given in Chapter 2 are drawn from contemporary letters and from autobiographical material in her book* Pearls from the Pacific.

*As far as possible, every detail has been checked for accuracy against contemporary letters, S.S.E.M. records, diaries, and contemporary issues of the mission magazine,* Not in Vain. *The author has spent many hours gleaning information from Solomon Islanders and from mission personnel, past and present, asking them to check the facts, opinions and descriptions recorded in her notes. Every attempt has been made to verify the authenticity of the events described.*

Fire in the Islands *is written for Islanders, for those who are deeply interested in what has happened, and for friends of the mission. As they read the story, perhaps many more will become interested in what God has done and is doing in the Solomons.*

# Introduction

I have long had connections with the South Sea Evangelical Mission. Dr. Northcote Deck was one of my father's closest friends, and the magazine, "Not in Vain," was a family periodical. While still at school, my brother and I planned to go and work in the Solomon Islands.

But other doors opened; I went to North Africa to work among the Muslims and for many years I lost touch with the S.S.E.M. Then one day last summer, when I had just returned to England, Alison Griffiths brought me the manuscript of this book.

I read it all day—partly because I could not put it down. I was drawn on from chapter to chapter. The things I read about seemed a far cry from our peaceful Warwickshire garden, but the message was relevant and right up to date. It speaks of that release of power for which we work in areas that still seem relatively barren, such as the Muslim world, and I laid down the book with mingled praise and yearning. Praise for what God has done in the Islands; yearning for what we believe He will yet do before our eyes in answer to believing prayer.

I hope that many Christians who read this book will be burdened to pray more deeply than before for a reviving work of the Spirit in their own immediate circles. Our Lord does not repeat Himself—He creates no two stars, no two snowflakes alike—and the manifestation of His power may be quite different in differing circumstances, but the old Biblical rules for revival are unchanged. In this simply-written narrative we see the principles of revival blessing traced to their source, when a young girl was led by the Spirit to care and pray for and teach a group of Island laborers generally considered beyond the social pale of that period; and who, disregarding convention and public opinion, gradually came to give her whole life to the service of their redemption. God always honors this sort of fearless, devoted obedience and the stream of blessing has been flowing ever since.

So I hope that many kinds of people will read this book: the old, who have more time to pray; the Christian workers who need encouragement; the faithless, so that they may marvel and be convinced; and the young, so that they may realize what a life wholly devoted to God from an early age may achieve. Let us all together praise God that He still works in power as He did in the days of Pentecost. I pray and believe that God will use this book to others as He used it to me.

*Patricia St. John*
*October, 1976*

*Glossary*

**Akalo**   An "ancestral spirit," according to animist belief; an evil spirit, according to Christian Islanders' belief.
**Atua**   A spirit-being worshipped by the Polynesian people of Rennell and Bellona Islands.
**Betelnut**   Fruit of the areca palm, chewed as a stimulant.
**Biu**   Communal house specifically for the men.
**"Bush people"**   Those who live in the jungle and live off crops of root vegetables, such as taros, yams and sweet potatoes.
**Fata'abu**   Animist priest or "witch doctor."
**Fetish, or "custom charm"**   Inanimate object, such as a piece of bark, worshipped as having magical powers.
**Kanaka**   Pacific Islander (specifically one working on a plantation).
**Localization**   Policy of giving the nationals the responsibility for their own country.
**"Saltwater people."**   Fishermen who live in lagoons on small, often artificial, islands.
**Tamberan cult**   A form of animist worship in the Sepik district of Papua-New Guinea.
**Tambu (taboo)**   Under a ban, forbidden or consecrated; prohibition based on religious observances.
**Yaws (Framboesia)**   Contagious disease causing open, weeping sores which may cover the body.

Sepik R.
PAPUA NEW GUINEA
SOLOMON
ISLANDS
QUEENSLAND
Bundaberg
AUSTRALIA
Brisbane
N

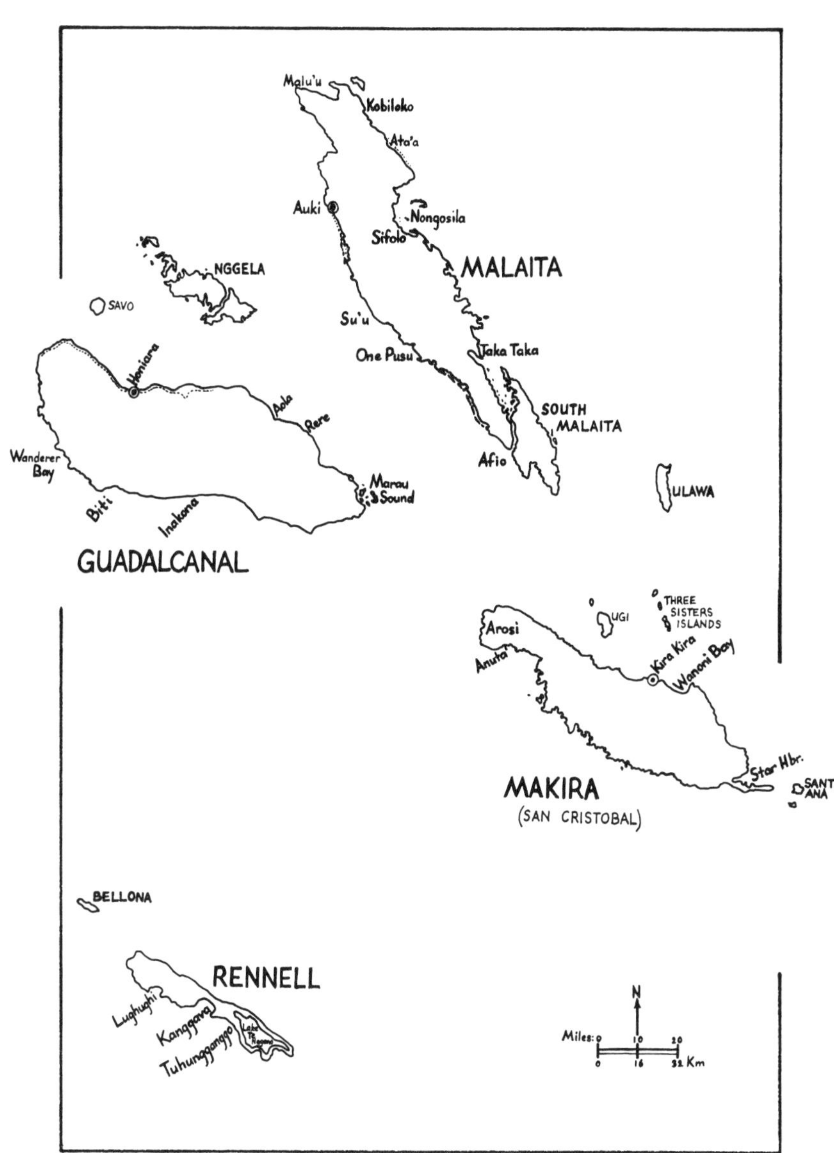

Malu'u
Kobiloko
Ata'a
Auki
Nongosila
Sifolo
MALAITA
NGGELA
SAVO
Su'u
Honiara
One Pusu
Taka Taka
Aola
Rere
SOUTH
MALAITA
Wanderer
Bay
Marau
Sound
Afio
Biti
Inakona
ULAWA
GUADALCANAL
THREE
SISTERS
ISLANDS
UGI
Arosi
Kira Kira
Wanoni Bay
Anuta
Star Hbr.
SANTA
ANA
MAKIRA
(SAN CRISTOBAL)
BELLONA
RENNELL
Lughughi
Lake
Tegano
Kanggava
Tuhunggango
N
Miles: 0    10    20
0    16    32 Km

# 1

# A
# God
# of
# Miracles

"Can you hear me now?" asked Jonathan Manepuri slowly and clearly, after the little group had prayed.

He was aware that any answer at all would be a miracle. Wawai, the young Solomon Islander before him, had never been able to hear or speak. All languages were unknown to him, and he could only call wordlessly.

Wawai's dark eyes were suddenly alight with understanding. "Yes!" he replied plainly, in their own language.

A surge of joy stirred the little crowd around them, and Wawai could hear, for the first time, the sound of their voices mixed with the new sounds of village life: a dog yelping, palm-leaves rustling, a child crying in the distance. The faces around him were full of excitement, and he could hear and somehow understand the words Jonathan was saying now:

"Then—praise God!"

It was 1970, and God was doing a new thing among His people in the Solomon Islands. Jonathan and the other expected God to answer their prayer and open the ears of the deaf. He had given them faith, and they knew He could work miracles; they had seen so many.

Spreading like fire throughout the Solomons were Islanders like Jonathan and those with him, impelled to share what God was doing. They had seen His Spirit poured out in full measure and had come to know His transforming power.

They remembered Kobiloko, where the church was filled with Islanders, tears streaming down their faces as God's holy presence overwhelmed them, till at last their weeping turned to joy.

They remembered the time at Sifolo—who could forget it! —when the hushed crowd of 2000, praying in silence, heard a sound coming from heaven like a rushing mighty wind, and it filled the whole place where they were sitting.

They had seen people broken, melted and cleansed by the Spirit of God—people who for years had been cold and hard towards Him.

They had shared in the singing and joy of praise which had flooded their being. They could not wait to share with others their discovery of all that God has in store.

Time and again they had seen God deliver people who were possessed by evil spirits. They had come to know first-hand His strong rescuing power.

They had seen the blind receive sight, and the lame throw away their tough, knotted sticks. Healed by God, those men and women could now walk the slippery jungle tracks un-aided.

They knew of marriages healed and the lives of young rebels transformed. Wrong attitudes, resentful thoughts, hurt feelings and jealousies were not beyond the reach of God's almighty cleansing power.

In their own lives, they had found a new hunger for God's Word, and a new reality in prayer. They had become sensi-tive to the spirit who is holy, and they knew they could hide nothing from Him. From their hearts they wanted to be transparently honest and open before God and before each other.

At that time, late in 1970, revival in the Solomon Islands had only just begun. There was much yet to be unfolded, still unknown to them, hidden in the future.

But the story, the full story of this mighty work of God, began a long time ago, when the people of the Solomon Islands were utter strangers to the Holy Spirit of God. In those days, the only spirits they knew anything about gave orders for a very different kind of life.

Every detail of daily living, from food-growing to fighting, was guided and controlled by the "ancestral spirits".

Deaths were blamed on sorcery and had to be avenged.

Skill in murder was prized.

One man killed and ate his own wife.

Childbirth was an ordeal that each woman faced alone, lest the spirits be angered and bring sickness and death on the tribe.

A young mother would listen in fear to the sound of her newborn baby's crying. She knew what would happen if it cried too much on the first night of its life, or if it was sickly. The verdict was always the same:

"The child kept crying. You know what that means. You must bury your baby alive and leave it to die. That will break the spell. If you don't, then every child you bear from now on will die."

In fear and anguish, she would scoop out a small hollow, lay her child in it, and cover it with a little mound. She had to obey; there was no choice.

For such lives to be re-made seemed an impossibility, but God is a God of miracles. The story of His transforming work in the Solomon Islands is the story of a miracle that spans 90 years. He began, surprisingly, 1000 miles away, in Australia; and every step forward from that strange, small beginning was a part of His total plan.

*Florence Young*

# 2

# "Come Help Me"

Across the cobalt blue of the sea, Peter watched the schooner glide through the gap in the reef. It was coming into his harbor at Malu'u on the island of Malaita, and he heard the shouts of excitement around him. Men were running down from the jungle to the beach of white sand near his hut, and some were already jumping into their sharp-nosed canoes. Their relatives were coming home again after three years or more on the Queensland sugar plantations in far-away Australia.

As Peter watched the crew cast anchor so close to his home, a great longing welled up in him. If only he could send a message to those he knew in Queensland! He had no pencil, and nothing to write on; but he might find something on board ship.

His canoe skimmed across the water; he tied it to the anchor-chain and scrambled up over the gunwale. As he talked to one of the crew, he saw an empty hessian sack tossed into a corner. That would do! Using red betelnut juice as ink, he wrote with his finger on the sacking: "Come help me. Peter Ambuofa."

He rolled it up and tied it with a scrap of loia cane. "Could you give this to Miss Young, at Fairymead?" he said to a returning laborer.

A thousand miles away, the message finally reached its destination. The people in Queensland who knew Peter read the brief appeal. They realized that the Christian message they had shared with him was taking root in the Solomon Islands.

Even into the last century, those islands were inaccessible, unwelcoming, notoriously wild and dangerous. How could God, who so loved the world, begin to reach into that corner of it called Malaita?

He began in a most unlikely way, in an old wooden shed on a sugar plantation in Queensland, north eastern Australia. Twelve years before Peter Ambuofa returned to the Solomons, a young woman, Florence Young, nervously faced her first class of Pacific Islanders. There were ten hefty men, and the house-girl. She looked at their names—which she had written on cards and hung on string around their necks —and asked her first question.

It was 1882, and Florence was visiting Fairymead, her brothers' new sugar-cane plantation near the town of Bundaberg. For the first time in her life, her close neighbors were people of a different race; men from the New Hebrides and the Solomons (isolated groups in the Pacific Ocean) who were employed as cane-cutters on three-yearly contracts. These were not the vague targets of those distant foreign missions she had found so boring at home in Sydney; they were flesh-and-blood people right there on the family property—laughing, smiling, gambling or fighting.

Florence found herself caring about these people. It was not right to leave them ignorant of the life Christ had in mind for them. She became convinced that God wanted her to teach these Pacific Islanders, no matter how inadequate she felt. So she taught that first Sunday class, telling them about life after death. In her hand she held a butterfly chrysalis as a living illustration of the new undreamed-of life that can emerge from the old earthbound shell.

Back again in her brothers' new house, she wrote a letter to her sister in Sydney: "Could you spare that *large* reading book Connie used to learn from? . . . I have begun a class of ten boys. I am afraid they don't understand very much and I don't know *how* to teach them 'ideas', but they seem very willing to learn."

She paused, and looked out at the fields of tall, waving sugar-cane where the men worked. It was not easy. The only way to talk to them was in Pidgin English, the trade language used on all the plantations, which she was learning to speak. There was no time to learn their various languages or to teach them English. They would be gone in three years and might never come back.

Feeling her way, Florence taught them as well as she could, explaining key verses in the English Bible, such as John 3:16—"For God so loved the world that he gave his only Son that whoever believes in him should not perish but have eternal life." The Islanders studied their carefully marked New Testaments, with the chosen verses underlined, and taught their friends.

At first, the little class hardly seemed important to the new settlers at Fairymead. What really loomed large was the state of their sugar cane crop, browned by the frost and threatening their financial ruin. Florence wondered if her brothers would still be there in a year's time. Not for a moment did she dream as she taught these men that this was the seed of a future Church in their far away island homes. The Islanders seemed to like their classes, however, and as their numbers grew Florence stayed on at Fairymead and it became her home.

The world of the sugar plantation became part of her life: the tall gums and the grassy river flats, the clangor of the crushing mill and the sweet smell of molasses, the cane ten feet tall and the Islanders hacking at the base of each stalk with their massive hooked knives. It was hard work, cane-cutting—stooping all day in the hot sun, slashing into the stems till trousers and shirt were stiff with sticky juice and caked black. Each man had a file at hand for sharpening his knife, and a sweat-rag round his neck. As thirst would overtake them, the men would stop for a swig from the water-bag that hung in the nearest shade.

At night they trudged back to their cluster of humpies in the Bush Paddock, glad to have a meal and a good night's sleep. When Sunday came, Miss Young's "school" was at least something different, even if it demanded mental concentration which they were unused to giving.

Jimmie Aoba was one who came, and as he listened, month after month, something began to come through to him. He still could not quite understand it all, but he wanted to find out more.

One day, in 1885, he stayed behind after the lesson. He wanted to belong to God, he said, and he wanted to learn more quickly. Once a week was not enough.

So Florence began an evening class. Jimmie would come, with a friend or two, and they met in odd places like the wash-house or the veranda—anywhere quiet. Very soon he was ready to hand over his life to his new Master, and he prayed very much for the other men at Fairymead who came from his own island of Aoba in the New Hebrides. Jimmie died from TB later that year, but within nine months twelve of his Aoba friends had become Christians. They were among the first to be baptized, in April and September 1886.

That same year, 1886, Florence began to feel a great longing to extend the work to other plantations. About 80 men came every Sunday to the class, and 40 came each evening; but, as Florence and her friends, and family knew well, there were 10,000 altogether in Queensland: imported laborers or "kanakas" as they were called.

Florence and those who shared her concern sent out a circular letter to all the Christians they knew, explaining the facts and needs. In Sydney her sister showed the letter to George Müller, who was visiting Australia at the time. He was a man who knew about prayer and faith. Without ever asking anyone but God, he had been given, over the years, more than a million pounds for his Orphan Homes in Bristol.

He read the letter quietly. "I think the Lord wants me to help this work," he said, and gave two guineas. "Tell your sister to expect great things from God and she will get them."

His gift was the first contribution to the Queensland Kanaka Mission, which came into being that year.

In January 1887, planters in the sugar-growing area near Fairymead were reading an unusual letter:

"To the Employers of South Sea Islanders in the Bundaberg district.

Dear Sirs,

Having secured the services of Mr. C. Johnson as a Missionary to the Kanakas in this district, we now appeal to you for sympathy and co-operation.

*The aim* of this Mission is, by God's help, to bring to those who are yet in darkness the glad tidings of the Gospel, in obedience to our Lord's command. (Matt. xxviii. 18-20)

It will be supported by the *free-will offerings* of those who wish to help in the work. Subscriptions will be thankfully received by the undersigned, but we wish it to be distinctly understood that no one will be pressed to give.

What we do ask, is, your help in providing facilities for the classes we desire to have on the various plantations. We propose that the Missionary should hold a class every evening and 2 or 3 on Sunday. Thus, by arranging for 8 or 9 central, weekly classes, a great number of Kanakas could be reached. Any further information required can be obtained from the Secretary.

Hoping the Mission will accomplish a great and good work amongst the Kanakas,

We beg to remain,
Yours faithfully,
E.E.B. Young
F.S.H. Young
Hon. Secretary & Treasurer
'Queensland Kanaka Mission'

*Address*
Miss Young,
  Fairymead,
    Bundaberg."


Whatever the local planters thought about the letter, they received Mr. Johnson and his wife very kindly and were perfectly willing for classes to be held. "Hope you have plenty of singing," they would add. "Anything to amuse them! But those kanakas can't learn anything, you know. Not that sort of thing. They just won't be able to grasp what you're talking about."

The pessimists were wrong, and three years later they freely admitted that the teaching was making a beneficial impact. Many Islanders attending the classes showed a transformation: their lives had changed direction.

About this time, somewhat to her surprise, Florence Young found herself unmistakably called by God to China. For most of the time between 1890 and 1900, others cared for the Q.K.M. while she was with the China Inland Mission. Those years brought her adventure, sickness and spiritual battles, culminating in the fierce dangers of the Boxer Riots. Looking back later, she realized that all this had been God's training school, preparing her to lead a pioneering work far beyond her expectations.

Meanwhile, the Q.K.M. gradually extended its work to other plantations, reaching thousands of Islanders scattered over a huge area of north-eastern Australia. New members had joined the mission staff, and they taught regular classes; but so did Islanders on many plantations. Having found Christ, they longed to introduce others to their new Friend and Master. Sometimes they would go on purpose to work on a plantation where there was no Bible class or "school," as they called it. After working all day on the canefields, they would gather together a group of their fellow-laborers for a regular evening class.

Sometimes a missionary would visit them to help and encourage and perhaps he would tie up his horse to a stump among the gum trees outside, and greet the Islanders gathered round a log-fire in the moonlight. Some of their work-mates would still be inside the cane-thatched humpies nearby, so missionary and Islanders would invite them to join the class.

The largest of the huts would serve as a classroom here, with its wide passage between the double row of bunks. In the dim smoky light of the kerosene lamps, the brown bodies of the crowd of Islanders would melt into the darkness, except for the gleam of white teeth and shining eyes. Only the volume of their singing, deep and musical, would give the missionary any idea of how many were present.

In a class like this, one man told 200 others how he had first come: "I used to hear a noise inside one house, and they told me about the missionary's class. I was frightened to join in, but I would creep up to the door on my toes and look inside. One time I saw a picture on the wall: a man, with a kind face, hanging on a piece of wood. I was very frightened. Then Dick Erromanga saw me and said, 'What are you looking at?' I told him, and he put his arm around me and took me up close to the picture. 'That is the Son of God' he said, 'Who came down from heaven to die for sinner man.' I kept looking at that picture for more than one hour. The missionary told me more about the love of God, and about what this Man did for me. God spoke to me through that picture and through that teacher, and I gave my heart to Him".

Through the teaching in those classes, over the whole sugar-growing district, thousands of South Sea Islanders came to understand God's claim on their lives, and many responded. By the time the mission could look back on 25 years of service in Queensland, there were 19 missionaries working in eleven mission centers, and 2,484 converts had been baptized.

In 1900, however, the shadow of change began to hang over the mission. The new Federal Parliament was considering a Bill to restrict the recruiting of labor, and to establish a Restrictive Immigration Policy. Increasing agitation eventually led to a government decision: all Islanders were to be sent home from the plantations by 1906.

It looked like the end of the mission: its field of service would be gone forever. Islanders who were mere "babes in Christ" must return without any shepherds into desperately difficult situations. They knew only too well what they would face. They remembered Tommy Ulleerutha, killed soon after his deliberate return to Malaita to share his newfound faith. Many of those in Queensland were to meet the same fate.

As the time drew near when they must leave, a powerful spirit of prayer came upon them. They prayed as they had never been heard to pray before. At night, they would stride out into the canefields where they could be alone with God. It was quiet there—with only the rustling of cane-tops in the wind. Looking up through the dark leaves to the night sky, they would pour out their hearts to God.

Alone or together, they prayed: "We hear the cry of our people in the South Seas, but we must have Thy fire burning in our hearts before we go home. Lord, send us the fire." They prayed for those who taught them, and for those who had already returned to the Islands. to "work with God in the dark."

They welcomed holidays as prayer days, glad to spend

**22**

every moment they could with God. Looking back later, it seemed that the Holy Spirit was revealing Christ in all His glory to them, in preparation for the battle which lay ahead when they returned to their islands.

As they departed, during the last few years, they carried with them the burning desire to stand firm for their new Master, and to share what they had discovered with their people. One said as he left, "My brothers, don't be afraid if you hear news from our country that the six of us have been killed. You rise up quickly and take our place."

The mission staff were very burdened; what should be the next step? Pathetic appeals for help were being received from Christians who had returned to the Solomon Islands and had made a brave beginning in sharing Christ with their own people.

Further messages came from Peter Ambuofa, who had chosen to return in 1894 to share Christ with his people at home. "I like you to come with missionary" he wrote one time. He could have slipped back easily into the old way of life, but instead, he braved hunger, loneliness and rejection by his own family for the sake of the message he brought.

The people of his island were animists, believing firmly in a supernatural world of unseen spirits. Their daily living was tied up with the strict observance of *tambus* or regulations and the appeasement of the *akalos* (ancestral spirits). To become a Christian involved a clean break from all this. For a man to continue living as a Christian in an animist village without observing these *tambus* was not acceptable; both sides recognized it as impossible. The Christian knew that he would be blamed as the cause of accidents, illnesses and crop failure; the animists knew that their *akalos* would be angry if they had someone living with them who refused to share in their worship and to obey their *tambus*. Therefore, from the start, Christians had to live separately. Ultimately they formed their own Christian villages, well away from the animistic environment.

At the end of the last century, practically nobody on Malaita knew anything of Christianity. Every aspect of life there was bound up with animism, which lay behind the blood-feuds, the sorcery, the murders and the cannibalism.

Anglican and Roman Catholic missionaries were already established in some parts of the Solomons, and the Methodists had just begun work in the western islands. Malaita, however—by far the most populous island—was almost untouched, and it was to Malaita in the Eastern Solomons that many of the plantation workers had returned.

*Peter Ambuofa*

# 3

# Peter
# on
# His
# Own

At the northern tip of mountainous Malaita in the Solomon Islands, the jungle plunges to a strip of harbor sand lined with coconut palms. This beach at Malu'u was Peter Ambuofa's home district. The date was July, 1894.

Down the steep jungle track, people from the inland villages were carrying their goods to the coastal market. The men held spears or clubs while the women were weighed down with bundles of taro and yams wrapped in plaited coconut-frond containers that hung from one shoulder. In their hands they carried clusters of bright green betelnuts, and hollow lengths of bamboo full of smoked nali nuts.

Already, the "saltwater" people were skimming across the harbor toward the mainland market in their canoes, pointed paddles flicking up spurts of water. They came from the small coastal islands to exchange fish for the garden produce of the "bush" people. Tucked into the narrow prow and stern of each canoe were bundles of fish and shellfish, wrapped in broad, green leaves.

The market was a clutter of bundles and people spread out on the ground, with a buzz of chatter and shrill bargaining. No-one wore any clothing, except perhaps for a bunch of twisted fibers in front, but body ornaments were plentiful. Muscular arms were adorned with shell bracelets and woven armbands, and sharp pieces of polished bone were thrust through cartilage to decorate noses. Half-moons of gleaming shell hung round the necks of some of the men, while others sported necklaces of human teeth or the fine, sharp teeth of a porpoise. Pigtusks dangled on their chests, and cowrie shells or red hibiscus flowers showed up against their dark frizzy hair. Near their womenfolk, the men stood ready with their spears, axes and old muskets, knowing that a fight could start at any time.

In the gathering throng, three men stood together—Peter Ambuofa and his two friends, Robert and Billy. They had arrived from Queensland a few days earlier and had found four boys on the beach looking for crabs. Peter had sent a message with them to his parents, asking that they come and see him, and now his keen eyes examined every person coming down the narrow hillside track.

At last he saw the familiar figures: his father carrying the weapons, his mother laden with bundles, both peering through the crowd, searching for their son.

"Is that you, Ambuofa?" they asked, for he looked different. The years in Queensland had changed his whole appearance. His hair was close-cropped, no longer wild and shaggy; and his body was clean and clothed in a calico. There was something different about his face, a new expression that gave light to his strong determined features.

"What are you doing here?" came the next question. "We hear you bring something strange and new . . . what is this? What is the name of this person you talk of? Where does he come from?"

Peter began to tell them: "I am a voice of Jesus. . . ."

But the new ideas meant nothing; they wanted Peter to

come back and join in the community life again. His mother pulled out a piece of roasted taro and showed it to him.

"Son," she said, "you come back with us, up to our home on the hills. You see this taro? It's your food, but if you don't come with us, you will die of hunger."

She put the taro back in her basket, and did not give it to her son. This act was like a slap in the face to Peter, for he knew well the deep-rooted custom that demanded the sharing of food with relatives. How determined they were that he should give in and go home! Yet he knew that compromise was impossible. To be true to Christ in his own village would stir up the anger of the *akalos* or "ancestral spirits" against his family, as well as against himself; so he stood his ground, trusting that God would supply all he needed far better than any relative.

When news of the three men's return travelled through the hills and small islands, relations of Peter's two friends came to Malu'u and found their men. All too soon, the two gave in to persuasion and returned to their old way of life, and when they left him, their faith breaking down, it was a sad day for Peter.

By this time, the little food he had was finished, and there was nowhere to get any more. Two of the boys whom Peter had met on his arrival were staying with him, and they were fascinated to hear him talk about the land across the sea, but they were not much help to him as they were extra mouths to feed. When Peter was at his wits' end, God showed him a gnarled tree, the *nwanwa'o* tree, which bears small seed fruits on its "body" once a year, for a very short period. He picked these small fruits, cooked them in a section of bamboo over a little fire, and they all three ate the food. For six months this *nwanwa'o* tree kept on bearing fruit, and meanwhile Peter made himself a food-garden. An old woman gave him the plants: taros, fannas, yams and young banana shoots and when the crops were ready to eat, the *nwanwa'o* tree stopped bearing fruit. Peter recognized his food supply was miraculous, God's special provision for him, for the tree would not normally continue to bear fruit for so long, carrying immature fruit and ripe fruit together at the same time.

Having planted his food-garden, Peter began to try to reach his people. One day he climbed the hill track to his own village, and told the good news of Jesus to his own relatives. When he came down again, his younger brother followed him, and another boy, too, joined them. So now Peter had four boys to teach, though he himself was a poor reader and did not know much about writing.

Whenever his family came down and tried to force him to go back with them, Peter held on steadfastly, not forsaking the work of his God as his two friends had done. He prayed often, but he also felt the need of some visible evidence that God was there, with him. While he still had some paper, he wrote out John 3:16 on a small scrap, and fastened it up on a tree. He knew perfectly well that his people could not read, but he had the feeling that God could see it, and perhaps an *akalo* might see it and say, "Eh, a man belonging to God lives here! I'd better go."

One day he went to a heathen feast, where he preached the gospel and sang the hymn, "Jesus loves me, this I know." Next day a young lad arrived, saying: "I heard you sing that hymn yesterday, and I've come to stay with you and learn to know more."

Then tragedy struck: the young brother in Peter's care died, and his other brothers came and accused him of bringing "white man's devils" to kill them. Furious and fearful, they threatened Peter's life. Peter knew they meant it. Fear of the *akalos* far outweighed any family feeling. He knew that his life was in peril, day and night, from that moment on.

"But," he said, "if they kill me, I go to heaven. I'm not afraid to die."

Several times after this his life was preserved. Men would

lie in ambush, only to discover that Peter had taken another track. They would thrust a spear through his leaf-wall to his empty sleeping place; something had made him choose another spot. One night, armed bush men came near his hut —but saw a shining light which filled them with fear. Another time, heavy rain wet the muskets and powder of men who had come to shoot Peter as he was planting taro tops. Word got round that Peter's God was very powerful.

For four years there was little to encourage Peter—until the time of drought. The bush people saw their own gardens wither in the heat, while Peter's garden flourished, with green leaves and thriving food crops. The men said, "Peter must have a powerful God to make his garden grow like that. We'll try sending down some of the women for him to teach, and see if they die or not. After all, they're only women". So they sent down women and children to learn from Peter about his new God.

The next encouragement was the return from Queensland of Christian men such as Silas Dindi and Charlie Lofea, who stood by Peter in his work for God. Together they would go up the hill into the jungle, away from all other people and noise, to pray and remember God's promise given to them in Queensland: that the sufficiency of God was enough, and that the island of Malaita would one day be His.

Meanwhile, Peter had been writing to Queensland, sending his appeals for help, but the Q.K.M. was not yet prepared to take on the daunting task of opening up a missionary work in the Solomon Islands. However, Charles Pillans felt the urgent appeal as God's call to him, and breaking his connection with the Q.K.M. he made his way in 1900 to Malu'u, unsupported by any missionary society and with equipment and provisions that proved inadequate. His letter gives a fascinating glimpse into what must have seemed like another world:

Dear Peter received me in tears of joy . . . and that

meeting on the shore I shall never forget. These three have certainly done much for Christ here . . . such as a white missionary would fail to do in such a time and under similar circumstances.

I have found our brothers well except Peter who has an attack of fever now and again. He says this has come on to him since his return from Queensland . . . Peter has a wife and one little daughter, Ruby . . . He is much respected and loved by these people here, and Silas and Charlie have work for the Master some miles from here.

They have been so busily occupied in their bread winning, that the school and missionary house were not prepared, Peter holding school in his house, such as it is, plenty of smoke, and oh, there are pigs too in the house; yet there is plenty of fresh air. . . . His pupils are numerous and most hearty; they love their school and the hymns, and are hungry for more. There are a large number of boys, young lads who are getting on, and God seems to have sent me here as a confirmation of His children's teaching, and to be a comfort and help to them.

We had an early morning meeting this morning under a lovely palm tree, and all around Peter's house are the pawpaw trees growing, and pineapples too. Oh, this is a beautiful place, the native parrots and birds of different kinds, screeching and singing in the forest trees—and the roaring waves on the coral reefs. . . . A small mountain stream opens itself into the harbour. The mountain streams are pretty and fresh, my joy and pleasure for two mornings has been to bathe before breakfast in this clear lovely pool amidst the trees and rocks and ferns. To reach Peter's place one has to climb a hill, up a path overgrown with the roots of trees, and much mountaineering has to be gone through to accomplish the undertaking.

I have been much struck with the humility, and love, and gentleness of these three dear Christian boys. As lights of the Master have they shone here for years past, and not without persecution. But white help is needed, too. Oh for a hospital here; so much sickness, medical missionary needed; cancer (perhaps tropical ulcers?) very prevalent, four cases here, limbs needing amputation, simply helpless . . . these folk have no means of helping in such circumstances, they suffer. I never saw such cases before, bone exposed in the leg of one boy, and others simply wasting away.

You would be saddened to see how hard the women work here. The huge bundles of wood and taro, etc., they carry; and the men too are not idle. Malaita people have to work, and no mistake. Taro is their chief food here; morning, noon, and night taro; now and again green bananas, boiled, and occasionally the fruit of the paw paw tree, and yams when in season. Their houses are all constructed of such material collected from the scrub and surrounding growth as they have through past generations found mostly suitable for such purposes. The fire is made outside (little or no wind to disturb the fire). Stones are heaped on and under and around the fire; those so heated serve to retain the heat for baking their taro upon. A roasted pig occasionally is a luxury, I understand. I do not know if I should relish such, for their feeding grounds near the locations don't warrant safety of partaking of swine's flesh here; yet hunger at times seems to know no bounds . . .

Sadly, unused to the local food and conditions, and succumbing to virulent malaria, Charles Pillans died within months of his arrival.

His friend, who arrived soon afterwards, went home seriously ill; and Frederick Schweiger, coming two years later, died at Malu'u. When Schweiger's companion also became ill, the British Resident Commissioner sent him home with instructions not to return unless supported by a mission society. These four men had each decided to go to Malu'u quite unconnected with any mission, in response to appeals for help.

What was to be done? In Queensland, as we have seen, the Q.K.M. had to face a whole new era because its chosen field of service was disappearing, as a result of the Restrictive Immigration Act passed in 1901. And in the Solomons, Peter Ambuofa and his Christian friends were still needing and asking for help.

For many years the Q.K.M. had been in close touch with the Rev. John G. Paton of the Presbyterian Mission in the New Hebrides and they now wrote to him, telling of the special needs in Malaita and asking that Mission to extend their work to cover the Solomon Island area. Though deeply concerned about the need, Paton replied that they were already fully committed and were unable to extend their work.

Approaches were then made to the Anglican Church Missionary Society, but Bishop Langley, after stating that the C.M.S. would be unable to enter that sphere, strongly advised the Q.K.M. to go forward themselves.

Those in the mission field felt intensely both the need and the responsibility. For months they prayed, and the sense of burden increased. The call became more and more insistent, until the conviction became clear: this call was from God. In January 1904, the Solomon Island branch of the Q.K.M. was formed, and a decision made to visit the Islands.

*"Saltwater" people*

# 4

# Into
# Coral
# Seas

The officer smiled across the table politely. "I don't think the Government will let you land on Malaita," he said.

"Oh, but I already have permission," Florence Young replied.

The officer still shook his head: "Not *there*—it's too dangerous."

He was right, of course. Malaita in 1904 was notorious. The Solomons had only been declared a British Protectorate in 1893, and the Resident Commissioner had been established at Tulagi just seven years. His job was to bring the wide, lawless area under control: a formidable task. He was extremely reluctant to let the two women in the group go any further.

"But in Sydney you promised!" Florence protested, with an inward urgent call to God for help. "And you can't send Mrs. Fricke back. I can hardly travel about with three men and no woman companion. Do let us go to Malaita in the *Daphne*, as we had planned."

Unwillingly, the Commissioner weakened and gave his permission. At least the little group of missionaries seemed sensibly equipped. On board the steamer they had brought with them a framed house ready for construction, six months' provisions, and a small sailing-ship, the *Daphne*, to transport them around the islands. These goods were unloaded at Gavutu Island, a trading station close to the island of Nggela, and the party prepared for the 60 mile sea journey to Malaita.

The purpose of the visit was to contact Christians who had returned from Queensland, and to establish one or two centers for mission work on Malaita. The two women would then return to Australia, while the three men planned to stay on. Hedley Abbott, O. C. Thomas and James Caulfield were to be the first missionaries sent out to the Solomon Islands by the Q.K.M.

On Friday, April 8th, the little *Daphne* was approaching Malaita, a long blue-grey land mass on the horizon. Ridges up to 4000 feet high run the length of this narrow island, covered by thick jungle. The ship skimmed past the waves breaking over Alite Reef, and threaded its way between small outer islets into the calm of Langa Langa Lagoon. A host of canoes immediately surrounded the little vessel, and before the anchor could be dropped, fifty Islanders climbed on board, clamoring for "toback." They were fascinated to see two white women, and urged them to visit their lagoon island homes.

Some of the islets were man-made, laboriously built up on the floor of the shallow, reef-sheltered lagoon. The "saltwater" people would collect coral boulders on rafts, and skillfully place them in position. When the mound of rocks rose well above high tide level, and sand filled the spaces between, it was ready for home-building. Ashes would soon make soil enough to support broad-leafed cabbage-tree palms.

The newcomers clambered from their dinghy on to one

over-crowded island that was home to 500 people. The villagers clustered around, smiling with blackened teeth. It was not the custom to wash, and their hair was never combed or cleaned. The married "saltwater" women were shaven-headed, and round their waists wore woven vines with fibers hanging down in front. The unmarried girls were naked, and so were the men.

Some of the people suffered from oozing, smelly yaws, and one had a tropical ulcer that stretched from ankle to knee. The bodies of some were entirely covered in the scaly, greyish fungus known as *bakwa*.

Stepping over children and pigs, the visitors made their way along the narrow alleys between the houses. They saw one woman suckling a piglet at her breast, till she jumped up at the sight of the strange newcomers—women with white faces and hands, wearing clothes that reached to the muddy ground.

Each house was small, with roof and walls of brown sago-palm leaves, and an opening that was only waist-high so that any intruder, stooping to enter, would be at a disadvantage. The missionaries had to bend low to go inside, and their eyes could see nothing at first, in the sudden darkness. There were no windows—only holes at each end of the ridge-pole, under the eaves, to let out smoke. In the dim light from the doorway, they gradually saw the cooking area at one side, with its fireplace and "oven" of heated stones inter-layered with broad leaves. Bundles of leaf-wrapped fish were cooking slowly, and the house was full of smoke that stung the eyes. Above the fire was a rack of firewood drying, and a few wooden bowls which the cockroaches kept clean. On the other side of the house were mats for sleeping on the earth floor.

Stepping out again into the brilliant sunlight, the visitors made their way back to the dinghy with crowds of pica-ninnies still fascinated by their clothes and white skins. As the dinghy pushed off, the children swam alongside, splashing excitedly.

The missionaries had much to think about, as night ended their first day on Malaita. In the darkness, Florence Young lay awake on deck, thinking of the people she had seen that day, the faces with no glimmer of light in them, the oppressive sense that powers of darkness were in complete control. Overwhelmed, she felt the task was almost impossible.

Next morning, the *Daphne* began the journey north-west along the coast for 50 miles. Rounding the northernmost point early on April 12, the little ship tacked eastwards, keeping well clear of the long reef that protects Malu'u harbor. It was a hot, cloudless day, and about noon the missionaries saw a big canoe heading towards them.

"Are they Malu'u people, do you think?" someone asked.

"Could be—yes, I think they are. They're wearing clothes. I say, we could let them know who we are. Let's sing something they'll recognize."

As the sound of a Christian song carried across the water, there was great excitement in the canoe. Spray flew from the paddles, and in a few minutes the Malu'u men were alongside. Their canoe was loaded with piles of taro and yams they were taking to Fo'ondo on the east coast. The Malu'u Christians had opened a new center there in 1903, and these men were carrying fresh food supplies to their friends working there. They were thrilled to see the missionaries from Queensland, and be the first to welcome them.

Leaving the canoe to continue its journey, the *Daphne* sailed on towards Malu'u. There was an entrance through the reef at the southeast end, and soon the little vessel was coming in to anchor just a stone's throw from the white beach.

Excited shouts spread the news of their arrival as four of the visitors climbed into the dinghy and rowed ashore. Strong brown hands steadied the boat while the two women stepped out on to the sand, and soon the missionaries were shaking hands with Peter Ambuofa at last.

He had much to tell them. His old parents and four of his brothers had become Christians, and 200 people came regularly for lessons each Sunday. The teaching of Jesus Christ was slowly but surely taking effect.

The missionaries planned to continue their journey down the east coast of Malaita, but all five were now suffering from attacks of malarial fever. They needed the help of skilled crew, and this was not at first available. At last some "saltwater" men from the Ata'a lagoon came to the Malu'u market, and they offered to sign on as crew next day.

That night, Florence Young could not sleep. She spent most of the time praying for guidance, and by morning she was certain that the east coast trip should be cancelled, and that they should return to Gavutu.

A little later, old Charlie Lofia came to see her. He had become a Christian in Queensland, and had returned to give his staunch support to Peter.

"Miss Young," he said, "I heard those Ata'a men talking. I know their language a little bit, and those men are no good. They're planning to run your boat on to a reef, kill you all, and rob the ship. Last night, I couldn't sleep. God was talking to my heart. He said, 'Charlie, you go on board the *Daphne* and look after Miss Young'."

So Charlie signed on as crew, with another Christian called Johnny. They were both bush men, with no understanding of boats at all, and only the third crew member, Peter Rai-ia, had any seafaring knowledge.

On April 20, the *Daphne* left Malu'u on the return journey to Gavutu, the trading station close to Nggela Island where they had first arrived by steamer from Sydney. All five missionaries were suffering bouts of malaria—shivering, sweating attacks of fever that left them weak and sick, unable to eat properly. Towards the end of the journey, O. C. Thomas—the only one on board who had any real knowledge of sailing—was helpless with a raging fever. Florence Young's account speaks for itself:

"We were becalmed from time to time, exposed to the merciless rays of a scorching tropical sun, for we dared not lower the sail to put up an awning. Every puff of wind was needed to stem the currents which might sweep us on to dangerous reefs. The glare from the sea added to the heat; and on the deck were two nailcans set in boxes of sand, in both of which fires were burning all day to cook rice for the crew, and boil the drinking water, etc. Our tiny craft had so little free-board that we could dip our hands in the sea over the low bulwark.

"We were a helpless party indeed. Neither Mr. Caulfield nor Mr. Abbott had had any experience in sailing boats. In the partial shade of the cabin deck-house lay Mrs. Fricke with a temperature of 106°, Mr. Abbott on the other side, 104°; Mr. Thomas helpless at the stern; both Mr. Caulfield and I very shaky and tottering. Thus as the sun was setting on the fifth day from Malu'u we approached the entrance to Gavutu harbour. There were no guiding lights, and we did not know where to anchor, so we crept slowly on, keeping to the right side of the harbour where there was less danger from reefs.

"By-and-by we asked Peter if the sails ought to be lowered. "Ask Mr. Thomas." We tried to rouse him, but he was half unconscious and only muttered, "It doesn't matter." So we still went on. Fortunately there was only the faintest breath of wind, for presently we crashed gently into the causeway between the two islands. This effectually roused Mr. Thomas for a few minutes, and his remarks were not complimentary to the duffers in charge! However, no harm was done, and with painful efforts we got the sails down and moored the boat alongside the wharf by 10 p.m. Next morning Mr. Caulfield endeavoured to take Mrs. Fricke to the house, a few yards from the wharf, while I tried to gather together the clothes and utensils we needed. Presently I thought I had better see how the others were getting on. I found Mrs. Fricke in a fainting condition half-way up the wharf. Mr. Caulfield and I together half led and half carried her to the veranda upstairs and for two hours one faint succeeded another.

"The trader left in charge of the store had been drinking heavily. He saw the *Daphne* approaching and took a heavy dose of chlorodyne to pull himself together, with the result that delirium tremens came on. That night his boys came to Mr. Caulfield for help, as he was missing. He was found on the reef without any clothes, and raving. We sent a note to Mr. Woodford at the Government Station at Tulagi, three miles away, asking him to take charge of the man. Poor fellow, he had been so kind to us before we left for Malaita; but none of our party were able to take care of him, and the second night he rushed round the house looking for knives, and for the two ladies! So we were thankful when Mr. Woodford took him to Tulagi, and that another of Captain Svenson's employees arrived in a small cutter and took charge of the store."

Six long weeks were spent at Gavutu, with recurring attacks of malaria. James Caulfield and Hedley Abbott recovered, but without O. C. Thomas they could make no use of the *Daphne*, and he was still helpless. A passing ship's surgeon advised that he return to Australia with the two women. On May 23 all three boarded a steamer to Sydney, still suffering severely from fever, while the other two men remained in the Solomons.

Sickness and hardship were not the only difficulties besetting this new venture; land was another problem. The brown-skinned men rejected by Australia's Restrictive Immigration Policy were extremely reluctant to sell any part of *their* land to a white man. Not even those who welcomed the missionaries could be persuaded to yield any land at first. However, by 1905 three centers were established: at Malu'u, Fo'ondo and One Pusu (ON-puss). The two missionaries were soon joined by a third, who in 1906 was allowed to settle on Nongosila, a tiny islet off the east coast.

Gradually, the transplanted mission began to put down roots in its new position, and to grow. New missionaries joined those in the Solomons, and among them was Florence Young's niece, Miss Kathy Deck, although her timid, gentle spirit hardly seemed suited to life in the Solomons.

Within a few years, two of Kathy's brothers had joined her on the mission staff. Dr. Northcote Deck left his medical practice in Sydney and launched into the work with complete dedication. A man of high courage, great charm and strong constitution, he was to become pioneer missionary, teacher, doctor, explorer and ship's captain—navigating the treacherous waters of the Solomon's group. His brother Norman gave up practicing dentistry to live by himself in primitive districts in the Islands. With his powerful mind and deep knowledge of Christian truth, he was to apply the Scriptures with quick insight to the needs of each community he visited.

Northcote and Norman were robust in body and spirit, but Kathy was by nature very sensitive. Strengthened by God, she was to become a woman of grace and wisdom loved by all, but the way ahead was hard.

*Kathy Deck*

# 5

# "Culture
# Shock"

These days, the correct term is "culture shock." In 1907, wave after wave of horror and compassion flooded through Kathy Deck's sensitive nature, but she had no name to give it. She only knew that this was life in the Solomons and this was where God wanted her.

Since 1892 Kathy had been part of the Q.K.M. in Queensland, but now that had finished, and the transplanted work in the Islands was to be called the "South Sea Evangelical Mission." The Islanders she had taught had returned to the Solomons and wanted help, so Kathy followed.

She was among the first to travel around Malaita in the brand-new yacht *Evangel I*. With its 20 h.p. oil engine to supplement its sail, it proved invaluable in exploring new areas and linking the centers of work. In this first visit, Kathy met many Islanders who were old friends—but their homeland was new to her, strange, sometimes terrifying. Her diary-letter gives us glimpses of events that stood out starkly in that first year.

"One Pusu, July 12: The *Malekula* came in, and brought the three refugees from Uhu." Kathy paused in her writing, and remembered the hunted look in their eyes. Polly and Piri were only young, not long married, and Piri's father had been shaken with terror. "All three were about to be killed and eaten when the ship rescued them, and, in order to pacify the people, a man threw out his young daughter, a girl of 14 or 15, to the murderers, by whom she was killed and eaten that night. The refugees will be safe here, we hope."

Three weeks later, the *Evangel* reached Malu'u to find the Christians there in great sorrow.

"What's the matter?"

"It's Charlie Lofia. He's been murdered. Four days ago."

"Tuesday evening he went down to the creek with his little girl, two years old. As he stooped to wash her face, five men surrounded him. They shot him four times."

"What about his daughter?"

"They clubbed the back of her head with the butt end of a musket, but she's still alive. A woman came running when she heard the shooting, and they shot her, too. She's recovering. But Charlie has gone; we have buried him. He was like a father to us."

Kathy felt the gloom and oppression hanging over the people, and the fear too. In the house on the hill where the visiting missionaries stayed, she threw open the doors and shuttered window spaces so she could breathe the cooler night air.

Suddenly she heard a cough at the door. It was John, an old Christian, very agitated, with a strong warning for the visitors.

"Why have you opened the shutters?" he asked. "You've got a light inside! Don't you realize that any heathen man could shoot you? He couldn't miss. We must pray that God will protect you, and you must shut every window." So they obeyed, but every night and morning the old man came to pray fervently for their protection.

By October, Kathy Deck was settled in the Nongosila mission house that was to be her home. Sheltered by reefs from the ocean's full force, the tiny island of Nongosila was linked to its twin, Kwai, by a sand-bar exposed at low tide. Even in her long white skirts on a hot day, Kathy could walk round the little island in 20 minutes—taking care to avoid the forbidden *tambu* grounds.

On October 26 she was sitting on the high raised veranda, writing home. Glancing up, she looked past the square iron water-tank, the coconut palms and the smooth green grass to the low coral wall that edged the beach. She stopped for a moment, thinking. It all looked so peaceful and beautiful, the motionless half-mile of sea, and the mountains of the mainland reflected in its green depths. What she was about to write seemed unbelievable. She dipped her pen in the ink again:

"The maternity customs here are very cruel," she wrote. "If the baby cries much the first night, or becomes sickly, it is buried alive. This is done to break the spell. It is supposed that otherwise all succeeding children will die. This has happened twice during our stay here, but we have only just heard of the custom.

"The last case was a little boy, a first child, and its mother buried it three times. Twice it writhed and cried; her heart failed her, and she took it out. But superstition gained the day, and the third time she completed the dreadful work by actually standing upon the little mound.

"We went to see her the next day, and found her looking very ill. When we touched her hand, we raised a storm of anger from the women who had brought us—they would all die if anyone touched her! We were not to come and see her again—no medicine or food could we send. If we attempted to see her, or even send a biscuit, we could not visit any of the villages for two weeks, nor could they visit the school. . . .

"We had much prayer, and this morning permission has come to visit the woman, on condition that we do not touch her. We fear she is very ill, and she is so frightened. Do pray for these poor creatures; they really love their children, but fear of the devil and of his spells holds them in terror and makes them act contrary to nature."

What Kathy did not know then was that though the woman would recover, she would never have another child.

There were many strict *tambu* rules surrounding a woman in childbirth. On Nongosila, when a baby was due, its mother had to build herself a small hut like a dog kennel in a segregated area for women only where she would live by herself for six weeks. During childbirth, she would be isolated and not even another woman could come within 50 yards. Her husband was not allowed to visit her for six weeks, and if she died, it was regarded as a sure sign that she had been unfaithful, and no one dared bury the body.

During her time in the hut, the woman was not allowed to store any food except taro, which does not keep, and she was dependent on her husband paying a young girl to buy food which had been grown in gardens which were *tambu* to men. Since the special food markets were held very infrequently, a new mother might even die of starvation.

On the mainland opposite Nongosila, midway down the east coast of Malaita, there was a regular food market held for bartering between the "bush" people and the "saltwater" fisherfolk. Kathy Deck could see the people gathering from her veranda:

"The saltwater people from Nongosila and Kwai gather on the beach outside the low stone wall enclosing the mission ground, and watch till they see the bushmen emerge from the scrub into the clearing opposite; then all hasten into their canoes and race across. The women carry on the bargaining—fish in exchange for taro and yams; the men stand near, leaning on their muskets and spears or shouldering axes."

The night before one such market, the local "saltwater" chief came to see the missionaries. "The bush people want to start a fight tomorrow," he said. "We want you to come with us. If not, we can't go. If you come, you can write a letter to the Government about any killing. They will listen to you. If you're there with us, I think those bush people won't start any fight. They don't want any trouble with the Government."

So next day, Kathy Deck and the others landed on the long beach that was alive with shouting, bargaining Islanders. Kathy recreates the scene:

"Reassured by our presence fearless and unarmed, they are mingling with one another freely, although several are making war-like demonstrations with their spears to show their prowess if need arises. We two ladies are almost torn in pieces by admiring women, and even the men want to touch our arms to find out if the white skin is real.

"When the bargaining is over, we begin to sing and Miss Dring and I take refuge behind the pictures, while dear red-headed John Selao preaches; otherwise we would distract the people. John trembles from head to foot, he is so nervous, but his eyes are full of fire, and his words pour out like a torrent."

About 500 people were on the beach that day; a seething throng of naked brown bodies, bundles of food, flaunted weapons. The air was tense with suspicion, each party fearing the other; and most were relieved when the market ended amicably. Not all, however. One old trouble-maker, seeing no prospect of a fight on the beach, had led a few men into an almost deserted village, and there they had killed a lame man.

In June 1908, Kathy wrote to her sister about a trip to Fo'ondo on the northwest coast of Malaita:

"Many heathen are leaving their mountain villages and coming in ones and twos to live with the Christians to learn of God. Two months ago a noted old cannibal came with two young sons. He is Joseph Furingalli's father."

The full story was extraordinary. Joseph's father, Korfenia, was a witchdoctor (*fata'abu*), an unkempt figure whose hair hung in long filthy strings. He was proud of its length, and of the fact that he lived in the men's *biu* and never ate food cooked by a woman.

He was reckoned to be a fierce fighting man in the bush, and had earned his wealth and his reputation by countless murders. Years before, he had killed and eaten his own wife. He sent his son for water to use in cooking her, and when the lad objected, his father threatened to kill and eat him, too.

The son ran away, found a ship going to Queensland, and recruited as a laborer for Bundaberg. There he heard the Gospel, and became a true Christian, taking the name Joseph at his baptism. On his return to Malaita, he found a mission station at Fo'ondo and stayed there. Sometimes he thought about his old father—but thought surely he was a hopeless case. In time, however, Joseph went to see his father two or three times; and now, this was the result— Korfenia was coming to "school" for Christian teaching, and to learn all he could.

And the miracle—the greatest miracle of a transformed character—had taken place. Korfenia now spoke to anyone he could about what had happened to him. His great regret was having so little time left in which to serve his new Master.

"Don't grieve about that," the Christians comforted him, "You came to Him as soon as you heard. You couldn't come any sooner."

"Last week," wrote Kathy, "his heathen people came down with strings of island money and many promises if he would only return." (Korfenia was their *fata'abu*, and they needed him desperately for their *akalo* worship.) "But he told them he now only wanted Jesus."

By nature, Kathy Deck was timid and fearful. Her sister

remembered her as a girl who was afraid of noises in the night; but her Master gave her not only His protection, but His compelling courage in the face of danger.

One time at Nongosila she was the only missionary on the island when Tabongi, a big Rennellese man, was left in her charge for five weeks to learn a little English. This Polynesian was a stranger in a strange land, and the local people became upset when he broke their customs. They attacked the Christian teacher, Joshua, who had been looking after the new arrival. When the Rennelese man saw them punishing his friend, he rushed at them with an axe in his hands.

"No!" shouted Kathy. "Give me that axe!"

She knew that if he so much as cut a man, he would be killed, so picking up her skirts, she ran to him and grabbed the axe-handle. The Rennellese was furious, and dragged her about, trying to wrench it free while she clung to it grimly, her hair falling down and her clothes tearing in the struggle. Finally, he tore the axe from her grasp, and vented all his violent energy in hacking down a coconut tree with a few mighty blows. Then, at last, Kathy managed to get the axe from him, and hid it safely under her mattress!

Being made of iron, this axe was extremely precious to the man from Rennell. Only a few months later, ordinary carpenter's nails and a few iron tools were to spark off a tragedy on the lonely island from which he came.

*Beach and Cliffs, Kanggava Bay*

# 6

# Where
# Iron
# Was
# Gold

Spears in hand and voices high-pitched in excitement, the great, husky Rennellese took their first look at the white man who had just scrambled out from under a house and was coming towards them. Dr. Northcote Deck was wearing a borrowed bark loin-cloth while his rain-drenched clothes dried, but above and below he was uncommonly pale. His fair hair was short and straight instead of long and bushy; he had no blue tattoos of fish and birds on his skin, and no smothering of pungent yellow turmeric. His eyes were blue —unheard of!—and his nose was narrow and straight above the trim mustache.

His hand was outstretched—was he trying to snatch a club? No, it seemed he just wanted to grasp a hand. Some kind of a greeting, perhaps, instead of rubbing noses in the usual way.

From Northcote Deck's point of view, this encounter with people cut off from the outside world was like a dream, unreal. On board the *Evangel* the day before, he had seen

Rennell, their island, looming up like a fortress, grey-green against the blue sea. Nearly 50 miles long and eight miles wide, this raised coral atoll towers 400 feet sheer from the ocean, with rugged cliffs encircling it like prison walls.

It was June 1909, and few white men had visited Rennell and its small neighbor, Bellona Island. The Polynesian inhabitants—tall golden-brown seafarers—had been left to themselves on their lonely islands 100 miles or more south from Guadalcanal, and Malaita, which are peopled by Melanesians—a very different ethnic group. Few Rennellese spoke even a word of Pidgin English and no-one knew their language. They were eager for contact with any passing ship, but few stopped because Rennell had nothing to offer—not even an all-season anchorage near its rugged, reef-rimmed cliffs.

As Northcote Deck and his two Malaitan companions clambered up the cliffs and started inland, they were guided by Tabongi, a Rennellese (with a few words of broken English) whom they had met on the shore. The rain poured down in torrents, so they sheltered for rest about midday in a clay-floored house with no walls, although the leaf thatch came down to a foot or so from the ground.

It was here that they met the excited Rennellese, with their waving mass of spears and clubs and long yellow arms. Word of the new arrivals had spread, and in smiling, eager curiosity, each side examined the other. But with no language in common, neither side could know just how dangerously different was their outlook on life. There was a gap between their cultures far wider and more ominous than could possibly be imagined.

Had they recognized it, a small hint appeared next day when the three visitors returned to the ship. Grateful for Tabongi's help in showing the way and carrying some of their gear, Northcote gave him an axe. He knew it would be most useful to the man, but he had no inkling of its worth in Rennellese terms.

The surface of Rennell Island is, for the most part, pure coral with scanty soil. Vegetation grows through the jagged grey broken lumps and hollows, with the roots of trees twisting down into the cracks and crevices. On all the island's length there were no stones or hard boulders, and to make a canoe took months. Painstakingly, the Rennellese would make a fire against the standing tree, then scrape away the ash with a shell edge. Time and again they would repeat the process until the tree was felled, then hollow out the log by making fires along its length. They had not even reached the Stone Age on Rennell! In terms of a white man's values, that steel axe was precious as solid gold—and Tabongi's chief wanted it.

As the visitors left the shore, they heard the fierce argument raging. Suddenly Tabongi broke away from the rest, leaped on to the reef and chased along after them, clutching his precious axe. He hurled himself into the ship's dinghy, and insisted on coming away in the *Evangel*. He seemed like a possible link with Rennell, and was left with Northcote's sister, Kathy, at Nongosila; but he was incurably homesick, a constant source of anxiety, and nearly died of pneumonia.

About two months later, on August 27th, the *Evangel* returned him to Rennell, and this time found a better anchorage in Kanggava Bay. Landing on the steep white beach, Dr. Deck climbed the cliffs and set off inland with three Rennellese guides and three Malaita crew. After a 12 mile trek, they came to the shore of a great brackish inland lake, clambered on to an outrigger canoe, and poled along the shore, in and out among the tiny islets. Again, there was that dreamlike sense of unreality.

"It seemed a world within a world," wrote Northcote later; "that inland sea, never before seen by a white man, those lake dwellers with their ancient customs, their canoes, their villages, living, dying, decaying, all unknown and unnoticed by the great outside world!"

Landing in a quiet cove, they spent the afternoon cooking

and eating, bartering for clubs, greeting new arrivals. Next morning, five massive, unwieldy craft sailed up majestically. The great chief, a giant of a man, had come from the far end of the lake. He greeted the intruders with grave dignity, and took them, on his barge, to the western end of the lake. From there they hurried overland—a long, hungry, weary journey—to rejoin the *Evangel*, their minds filled with the numbing strangeness of their experience.

Five Rennellese were prepared to come away on the ship to One Pusu—but they, too, found adjustment to life away from their homeland almost impossible. As a people, they had been too isolated, so, in following months, Northcote Deck made two more trips to Rennell, returning the five men and exploring the island further. Once, he crossed the lake and went on to the northern coast of the island. Another time, he trekked inland to a village in the central west. He was fascinated by the people and their customs: the two-foot wooden shark-hooks, the spears tipped with human bone, the lack of freshwater streams. The people seemed so friendly, like overgrown children clamoring continually for knives, axes, fishhooks and beads. With quite different customs of ownership, they took anything left unguarded: a belt, a pannikin, a broken bottle (for shaving). For anything metal they had an insatiable craving.

As Dr. Deck and his companions shared their discoveries, three Melanesians heard about the Rennellese and felt the call to share with them the Good News. Freely they had received, freely they wanted to give. As others had come to them, so they wanted to go to Rennell and share with the people what they had learned of God. Their names were Thomas Sandwich (a New Hebridean Christian of mature experience), Tommy Makira (from Makira) and Andrew Kanirara (from Malaita). Their offer to live on Rennell and learn the language seemed to answer the problem of getting through to the Rennellese, who could not adjust to leaving their own island but who seemed so friendly and welcoming.

On August 14th, 1910, the *Evangel* arrived once more at Kanggava Bay, bringing the three new teachers, their gear, and planks to build them a house. Miss Florence Young was on board, making her only visit to Rennell, together with Miss Dring. While Dr. Deck and the other men from the *Evangel* worked hard at building the house, the two women were invited by a chief Kungivai to visit his house, which he proudly displayed. At the time, he seemed genuinely delighted to make them welcome; not a trace of menace clouded the day.

Hurriedly, the house was built on the cliff top—one room, with an iron roof to catch the necessary rainwater, and a square tank to store it in. As the men worked, scores of smiling Rennellese surrounded them, fascinated. They saw the precious nails being hammered into the timbers—such a waste! What marvellous fishhooks they would make! No wonder Northcote Deck remarked: "We had to watch that the nails went into the boards and not into their pouches!"

Three days later, the *Evangel* set off again, leaving Thomas, Andrew and Tommy well stocked with rice, biscuits, and tools to make a food-garden, a natural, sensible provision. But iron was gold on Rennell. Those men of the Coral Age were crazy for it, and no-one—neither white man nor Melanesian—had any conception of the temptation they left on the island. Nails, tools, iron roofing, iron tank—and three foreigners who couldn't speak the language and who were quite unarmed. . . .

When the *Evangel* next visited Rennell some months later, Shadrach Amasia was one of the crew. As they came into the empty bay, Northcote Deck signaled with a double blast of dynamite, but there was no response. Then they saw that the house was gone, and three sheets of iron leaned against the cliff below.

Northcote took the dinghy ashore, leaving some crew members to guard it. He and Shadrach ran up the steep beach and climbed the track to the cliff top. On the way they found the old coat, now torn and rotten, which Shadrach had given to Andrew. Northcote peered cautiously over the crest, and saw the ruined house. Each timber had been split to get the nails, and the iron was gone.

Inside the wrecked house, they found the bones of Thomas under a rotting mattress. There was no skull, and the arm and leg bones were missing—to make those bone-tipped spears? They climbed back down the track, and underneath the cliff found the missing skull, fractured by a tremendous blow. Deeply disturbed and heavy-hearted, they rowed back to the ship.

Next day, the men on the dawn watch saw a canoe approaching diffidently. Northcote met the canoe in the dinghy, and found that the man was Temoa, who had been to One Pusu. They returned to the ship, and Temoa told them that all three men had been killed.

On the following day, they took him ashore. Gradually the local people gathered. The old chief Tepaika could hardly be persuaded that the men from the ship did not want to kill in revenge. As best they could, the Rennellese conveyed what had happened: three men from a nearby village had done the killing, led by Kungivai (who had shown Miss Young his house). They coveted the axes, tools and outfits left with the teachers, and killed the three men on the second day after the ship left. The people of Rennell as a whole were not responsible, but these three individuals: Kungivai, Maumau and Teketoa.

In the newly-started garden clearing, Maumau had brought Andrew a green coconut, then clubbed him from behind while he drank its juice. Teketoa had attacked Tommy at work in a far corner of the food-garden, and the blow caught him on the neck. He had run towards the house, then doubled down the hill again and rushed into the scrub, calling "Jesus, Jesus, save me!" so passionately that the Rennellese remembered and repeated his words. But he was a short, heavy man and he had no hope of escape. Near the

**60**

track, he was caught and killed. In the house on the cliff, Kungivai had brained Thomas with a heavy staff.

The heads of all three had been cut off, and their arms and legs split open to get bones for spearheads. Their bodies were left unburied in the sun; but they were not unmourned. The local women had their foreheads still cut and bleeding, the Rennellese way of showing grief. They told in sign language that the old chief had beaten the killers about the head and driven them inland.

Northcote felt that he should go inland to see the big chief of the lake concerning the killings, but news came that the chief himself was coming to the coast, so they waited. Instead, his son came, and for several days wilder men from miles inland gathered on shore, outnumbering those who could be counted friends. One day, despite attempts to limit the number on board the *Evangel*, canoes kept coming from which men would jump aboard.

Shadrach was convinced that the Rennellese wanted to kill them in order to get posession of everything on the ship. Without asking permission, he armed the crew with axes so that they could defend themselves and the *Evangel* if need arose. The crew were ten Malaita men, and there were no firearms on board.

The situation became very tense. Four outrigger canoes kept ferrying more Rennellese to crowd on to the *Evangel*, and it was necessasry to use the ship's dinghy to take some of them back to shore. One chief refused to go, and, as he was put overboard, tried to axe Northcote; but according to Shadrach's memory, Northcote then threw a stick of dynamite into the sea, and at that, everyone fled in fright. Forgetting the canoes, they swam for the beach.

When the Rennellese had gone, Northcote and others from the *Evangel* went ashore once more. They held a service on the sloping white beach, and buried the bones of the three teachers in the sand. Then the ship left; and, for many years to come, Rennell was a closed island.

*Heathen Islanders, Central Malaita*

# 7

# Where
# Death
# Was
# King

With the killing of Frederick Daniels, the year 1911 brought further sorrow to the mission. Frederick was the victim of the "payback" system on Malaita, where a man had to avenge the murder of a relative by killing the murderer or one of his kin. Any white man was regarded as the kin of any other white man, so Frederick Daniels was seen as a convenient member of the "white man tribe" to be killed in revenge for a man's death from sickness on a distant plantation years before. Being animists, the dead man's relatives reasoned that the "white man tribe" was, of course, responsible.

Not knowing that there was a price on his head, the young missionary spent four days in a tiny Christian village at Uru, six miles south from Nongosila. On the Sunday night the handful of Christians gathered together to sing praise outside in the cool of the evening, and Fred Daniels had just asked for one more hymn. He was sitting on a rock, with his acetylene lamp beside him, joining in the singing. Without warning, a gun was fired, and he cried out "Lord, save me!" He tried to stagger to his small hut, but collapsed and fell, with his songbook against the bullet-wound in his chest.

When they heard of their colleague's death, the other missionaries wrote immediately to the Government, explaining that they had all come to Malaita knowing the conditions and aware of the risk to their lives. However, as the authorities would probably consider it necessary to punish this crime for the sake of other Europeans, the S.S.E.M. asked that any punishment be for the actual murderers only.

This episode highlighted the clash between two cultures with opposing views on justice, but the differences in outlook went far beyond that. The Islanders were animists, and their beliefs permeated every part of their everyday life. Only someone brought up within this life framework could give an authentic insight into the animistic mind. Jotham Ausuta is such a man, the son of a North Malaita chief, brought up to follow in his father's footsteps as *fata'abu* or animistic priest. At the age of 12 he was sent to the mission for medical treatment, and later became a Christian; but his words demonstrate his first-hand knowledge about the old beliefs.

Before Christianity came, we already knew that there was a power which could do miracles. After receiving the gospel, we realized that those powers we had experienced before were not the powers of ancestral spirits, but the supernatural powers of the Deceiver.

Previously, we had thought that there were two forces: ancestral spirits or *akalos*, who would be good to us and help us; and unfriendly spirits, of an enemy kind, that we feared.

After Christianity came, we realized that these powers certainly exist, though they can turn and kill you if you follow them. We understood that the Deceiver, Satan, had organized two "teams" of spirit powers: those pretending to be helpful ancestral spirits, and those that were openly against us, enemy spirits, to frighten us.

An *akalo* or spirit power would come and speak through a *fata'abu* such as my father in a recognizable way. If the *akalos* were showing sorrow, the man would cry. If they were showing excitement, he would shake strongly.

The *akalos* would become angry if someone broke any *tambu* or rule forbidding some act. For example, a *fata'abu* while holding office may not eat with his wife and family. That shows his real devotion to the service of his ancestral spirits. If he breaks that *tambu*, he is insulting the *akalo*.

In those days, our people did not believe that any death came from natural causes. If someone in our house died, we always thought it must have been caused by somebody using enemy spirits to kill that man. The *fata'abu* would ask the ancestral spirits who was responsible and how the death had come about. Then the *fata'abu* would name the person regarded as responsible for the death. Relatives of the dead person would then offer blood-money as a reward to anyone prepared to kill the one considered responsible, or any of his relatives; so no one was safe.

We had to obey the *akalos*, because they could punish people. A man might go berserk, for example, and run around bashing himself and getting cut. Or he might get sick, or his piglets might die. When such things happened, we had to find out from the *akalos* what was wrong and how to appease them.

Through the *fata'abu*, the *akalos* could give special powers to people. For instance, a baby boy would be consecrated to the *akalos* one month after birth. As soon as it came back from isolation with its mother, the father would take his baby son to the man's house. They would have made special puddings so they could give the baby a little bit; and they would hold special ceremonies and mark the child with betelnut. Everybody knew that day, like a birthday. When the baby was brought in, all the men

**65**

would shout and give him a prepared name. If he cried at the shout, they would say, "He'll grow up to be a fighting man!" and they would invoke for him the special power for quick anger. If he didn't cry, they would say, "He'll be a peacemaker!" and claim for him that appropriate power.

Before Christianity came, the whole of our life, from food-growing to fighting, was controlled and guided by the *akalos*. Many people still continue in that old way, and I can understand why. Because we love our clan, our community—our fathers and ancestors—we count it a privilege to serve them. Until light comes, we don't know that those are not our ancestors' spirits at all, and that it is only the Deceiver, Satan, at work.

Sometimes people do forsake those old ways. Perhaps they see a miracle, or see that Christians are different and enjoy themselves without the burden of sacrifices demanded under threat. Perhaps they come to feel that the *akalos* are impossible to please, and so decide to try the new Christian way instead.

On Malaita it was almost always the islanders themselves who first strode boldly into "enemy-held territory" with the Christian message of release for the captives and illumination for those whom "the god of this world" had blinded.

One such was Abraham Wikau who lived at Hauhui Point between One Pusu and Su'u. One day Abraham visited a heathen feast, taking with him a picture of the Crucifixion. During the feast, at some risk to his life, he got up and preached the gospel in a clear ringing voice. All went well, and he returned home.

At that stage, since he had no converts yet, Abraham lived quite alone; so he tied up his door securely. That night there was a battering at his door, and a voice saying "Let me come in!" He opened the door to find Ofanidi, a tall, gaunt, desperate character holding a Schneider rifle. Abraham thought, "This is the end of me," for he knew that the man often killed on sight.

Ofanidi said, "You were at the feast. I heard every word you said there. I was hidden in the trees, and you spoke about a man called Jesus Christ. I've come now for you to tell me more about Him."

Abraham took the man into his house and taught him. Night after night, Ofanidi came back, and the teaching went on and on. Always he came at night, for fear of being seen, and finally he accepted Jesus Christ, and took the new name, Paul, in baptism.

Paul Ofanidi had been a great killer, feared and hated. He had killed and eaten over 60 people. He couldn't live among his own people because of their hate and rejection—they knew he had killed and eaten members of his own family. He was known to be quite untrustworthy, a criminal of the first order in a community of headhunters and cannibals.

As an outcast, he had lived alone in the jungle, feeding on roots and berries and anything edible he could find. He had always been on the move, sleeping at night in the boles of trees, because everybody was out to kill him as he had been out to kill them. He had even been known to dig up the body of a dead man and eat it; in fact, he had descended so low that apparently he was more like a brute beast than a man.

This was the man who had come and found Christ in Abraham's home. God had worked in his heart to take away the darkness, and as he sat in the house each night, he asked many questions—always with the door securely shut. When he accepted Christ, however, he left his gun with Abraham and went to the relatives of the people he had killed.

"You can kill me," he would tell them, "but I can't kill you."

All were so dumbfounded at the change in Ofanidi that they did not kill him. He became known as a Christian, living in a Christian village and going around telling others about the One who had transformed him.

*John Waite, Robert McBride, Northcote Deck, Mrs. McBride, Mrs. Deck, with Christian leaders.*

# 8

# One
# Pusu:
# The
# Powerhouse

To a very great extent, it was Christian Islanders who went out sharing the gospel with their fellow-countrymen, but those Islanders themselves needed and asked for teaching and encouragement. For many in the early years, "teaching" meant One Pusu, the mission headquarters and training school. Encouragement was given by the missionaries on their ship, *Evangel*, in its continuous round of visitation, and by outstation missionaries, who lived nearer at hand and kept in close touch with their local pastor-teachers.

In the early days, One Pusu was a haven as well as a school. In 1905 the mission headquarters was built there on a narrow arm of coral that jutted from the mainland, ran parallel to the west coast of Malaita, and enclosed a sheltered harbor where huge trees were felled and coconut palms were planted to grow amazingly well on the coral-based soil. The mission house was built on 15 foot wooden piles for safety (barbed wire discouraged would-be intruders from shinning up these poles) and the space below was used as schoolroom, church and store. Although for years a watchman was on guard at night, payback murders still took place within a stone's throw of the house. Once, a small boy was the victim; another time, a young woman was killed.

At first, the training school took almost any who would come. Later, when more Christian villages had been established, local teacher-pastors would recommend trainees who had been taught basic literacy. Most were single men who came for the two years' training. A very few were married couples.

One early student was Abel Aeakalo, a short stocky grizzled man with a strong determined face, the eldest of ten sons from the Langa Langa Lagoon and a clever man. In the center of Abel's nose a deep hole had been bored, a sign that he had killed his man. At last this murderer of three had come to a Christian village for teaching, and had found Christ. He went on to One Pusu to learn more. To teach such a man, the missionaries had a program, developed over the years, and in this, Miss Violet Sullivan played a most important part. The program used island languages, Pidgin English and some English. It sounds a strange mixture in which to teach eternal truth, but in practice it worked.

Abel would file into class and begin like a child to learn to read his own language. "Ka-ke-ki-ko-ku" he would read from the Syllable Roll and the language primer, mastering the basic sounds written phonetically. There might be men from 10 or 15 other dialects with him in the same classroom, so Pidgin English was extremely useful as a common language. Like *Koine* Greek in the time of Christ, it was a *lingua franca*.

Having grasped the elements of reading, Abel would move on to the *Question Book* which the missionaries had translated into eight languages or dialects parallel with the English text. This would become his first reading book and also his grounding in the profound truths of Christianity.

Beginning with 14 key passages of Scripture tracing the

road to deliverance, this small booklet spelled out such basic teaching as the Ten Commandments, the account of the Creation and Fall, Christ's birth, baptism and temptations, His calling of the disciples and His life on earth, being "born again", the Lord's Supper, His Crucifixion, Resurrection and Second Coming, the Lord's Prayer and the Creed. As simply as possible, each truth was put in the form of question and answer, as the very first question shows:

1. *Tell me one text where God says if we break one command we are guilty of all.*
   Whosoever shall keep the whole law, and yet offend in one point, he is guilty of all. (James 2:10)
   *What does "whosoever" mean?*
   Every one.
   *What does "the whole law" mean?*
   All God's commands.
   *What does "offend in one point" mean?*
   Break one command.
   *What does "guilty" mean?*
   Sinner.

Having inched his way laboriously through the *Question Book* in English alongside his own language, Abel would then begin the study of graded lessons in Bible knowledge now known as *Bible Outlines*. Like the Authorized Version of the Bible, this was in English, so each main point and difficult word had to be explained thoroughly in Pidgin.

Because the Bible is a most practical handbook for living, these Bible Outlines were often very much to the point. The earlier studies made clear and simple the basic teaching to be found in the giving of the Law, for example, or the account of Calvary. Later lessons included such topics as "Christian husbands," "Giving to God" or "How to care for our bodies."

Each lesson would begin with a reading from the Bible in English, and this was followed up by four or five points centered on the Scripture reading and carefully explained in Pidgin. For a whole week the same lesson would be given, day after day, and then on Friday the students would tell back the story and its meaning in their own words. It soon became obvious if they had not understood!

The very first time that the lesson on "Christian husbands" was given, a young married man called Asaph had to tell it back with his own interpretation. He said, "You husbands, you must not make your wife walk behind you like a servant. You must make her walk beside you. And even if someone you meet says, 'What, is your wife like a star that's fallen from heaven?' you must take no notice. You must be kind to your wife and even help her carry loads. It's not easy, but that doesn't matter. You know that chorus:

> 'If all were easy, if all were bright,
> Where would the cross be, where would be the fight?' "

Mind you, in all fairness, Asaph did have a difficult wife. Next day, he came to Violet Sullivan, his teacher, and said, "I couldn't sleep last night. All night, my wife talked to me about how to be a good husband."

"Oh," said his teacher, "Of course, she was in that class. Never mind, next week we'll be having the lesson on how to be a good Christian wife!"

Always at One Pusu there was more to learning and teaching than just the formal lessons. Any time of the day could bring opportunities for the kind of informal teaching that matters most. One day in the 1920's Kathy Deck's sister, Joan, was sitting in the house when she heard furious footsteps come stamping up and across the veranda. Through the door came Abel Aeakalo, his chest heaving and his face dark with fury.

"What's the matter?" Joan asked him, and he told of bad news from home. A man had wronged his family. Only his death could wipe out the disgrace.

"I must kill him, I must kill him!" said Abel vehemently, his eyes flashing, as he plucked viciously at the edge of the floor mat he was sitting on.

Just then, Kathy came in. She had worked for many years now among these Island people.

"You belong to Jesus Christ now?" she asked, when she heard Abel's story. "Is Jesus Master of you now?"

"Yes," he said.

"Well, now, Jesus told us something about this. He said, 'Love your enemies and pray for those who persecute you.' You must pray for this man who has wronged you. As you pray for him, God will give you the power to forgive him, and love your enemy. By yourself, you cannot find it in your heart to forgive this man. So you must pray."

Joan saw Abel's heaving chest quieten as he listened. He looked intently at Christ's words in the Bible.

"You mark it in my Bible," he said at last. With his great thumb carefully on the verse to keep the right place, he went off to be quiet with the Master. He had much to consider, and in the end he did what had seemed impossible; he forgave from his heart the man who had wronged him.

At One Pusu, the learning process was slow but thorough, and provided continuity of teaching. Solid foundations were laid and steadily built upon, week after week. Island Christians like Abel absorbed this method of teaching, and back home in their villages afterwards they followed that same method. Each day they gathered the people morning and evening—for a reading class and a Bible lesson—quite apart from the special services on Sunday.

After his two years at One Pusu, a student like Abel Aeakalo would be back to his Christian village, perhaps, as a teacher-pastor, or he might be called to another area as an evangelist. To give him a start, fellow-Christians might help him build a house and a tiny church, and plant a food-garden. Then he would simply live as a Christian in that place, and the local people would watch and see him consistently refusing to follow the old ways—the *tambus* and sacrifices to the *akalos* upon which they felt their lives depended. They would not dare let go their worship of the old spirit powers unless they could be sure that the God of this new Way could offer them power and protection, otherwise, the *akalos* would punish them.

It might be twelve months before the first inquirer came, and often this would be a man with terrible leg ulcers or some other sickness. His relatives would have sent him as a test case, to see if the new Way was powerful enough to counteract the anger of the *akalos*.

For Seth Mumaoma, not yet 20, the first year after his One Pusu training was hard and lonely. He went to live away up in the hills of Kwara'ae, completely alone, and when the missionary came to see him after that first year, he said proudly, "One person has just come a little while ago!"

There, living with him in his own house, was this one man, sent down to him with a huge, appalling, smelly ulcer. Seth was caring for him, washing his sore, feeding him, ignoring the terrible stench of the ulcer, and telling him about a new Master who truly loved him. The people around would observe Seth's care and faithfulness and patience, and they would see that the Christians had something different in their lives.

After watching a Christian's life for a while, a heathen man would come, perhaps because he had finally tired of sacrificing to *akalos* who still kept him in bondage, fear and misery. The Christian evangelist would tell him to finish up any feasts he might owe, and make a clean break with his past way of life. Then the evangelist would ask the newcomer to give up his ancestral bones, or sacred relics of any sort. Together with the man who had just come, he would pray specifically that the protection of Jesus Christ would be round about them; then the relics sacred to *akalo* worship would be desecrated. Together, they would build a house and plant a food-garden, and the newcomer would receive daily teaching in the Christian way of living and trusting God. Thus, gradually, a Christian village would form around the nucleus of the pastor-teacher's house and little church.

It was through an unassuming village pastor that the course of Maelalo's life was changed and One Pusu received a student who became in time an outstanding man of God. Maelalo was a young policeman, and one Sunday he came to shoot pigeons near the Christian village of Ambu (next to the present-day Auki township). Shadrach Marama, the teacher-pastor, asked him not to disturb the service because Sunday was the special day for worshipping God.

"I don't know about God," said Maelalo.

"Come back this afternoon, then," said Shadrach, "and I'll tell you about the true God."

Maelalo came—to listen for hours, asking questions, intensely interested. He attended the services on Sundays, received instruction eagerly, and came to believe in Christ as God's Son and his own Deliverer. Then he went to the Government official, asking permission to leave his job in the police force because he wanted time to learn more and to train for God's work. Once a week was not enough; he wanted thorough teaching every day at the One Pusu training school.

So Maelalo arrived at One Pusu, a tall handsome young fellow with a strong, alert face. Already he spoke fairly good English because he was a natural linguist and very intelligent.

"I come from Langa Langa," he said, and the missionaries were amazed and delighted. They knew very well that the people of the lagoons were strong forceful characters who held on to their kinsfolk tenaciously—especially their young men. Quite apart from the close ties of kinship, the "saltwater" people needed a certain number of hands to hold the huge fishing nets, 100 meters long, to draw in the catch for a feast. Fishing was their livelihood and the basis of barter with the "bush" people from the mainland. A "bush" man could grow food individually, but the "saltwater" people were closely interdependent and could not bear to lose anyone; yet here was Maelalo, a young man of exceptional promise, coming of his own accord away from his own people.

He told how he had visited his relatives to tell them he would be leaving them to learn more about God. A Christian friend from Ambu had paddled with him in the canoe, and held it while Maelalo went to fetch his belongings and say goodbye. Everyone converged on him, talking, dissuading— and step by step Maelalo backed away from them across the tiny islet, towards the shore. Suddenly he sprang into the canoe and paddled hard, cutting himself off from his old way of life forever. As his people very well knew, it was one thing for Maelalo to work for the police a few miles away, remaining linked to home by ties of duty, religion and kinship, but it was quite another matter for him to go away and take up a new way of life altogether.

At One Pusu, Maelalo began to cross the bridge from complete illiteracy to a deep understanding of the Bible, even though it was written in English. Although he was a grown man, he learned for the first time to read and write, using the simple primer and the *Question Book* in his own language. From there he went on to graded lessons in Bible knowledge, outstripping his fellow-students in his ability and eagerness to learn all he could about Christianity.

When Maelalo made public his faith through baptism, taking the name of Clement, that step cut him off completely from ever returning to live on his home islet, and from all rights of inheritance. Seeing this, his son a Christian, his father said angrily, "You are an old woman now. You cannot fight or kill. I'm finished with you!"

Clement Maelalo was outstanding as a student, a man quite out of the ordinary, but God also used "what the world calls foolish" in fulfilling His purposes. Just as Peter and John, Jesus' closest companions, were "ignorant, unlearned men", so were many of His followers in the Solomons.

Samson Jacko was a quiet greyhaired little old man when at last he made his visit to One Pusu. He had become a staunch Christian in Queensland and could read his big Bible a little, but he never learned to write. Returning to the Solomons about the same time as Peter Ambuofa, Samson worked alone among his people for 18 years. Few ships called at Inakona on the rugged coast of Guadalcanal, and no one but God knew what had become of him. With no book but the best, and no help to understand it but the highest, his faith was simple, strong, real, all-pervading; he wasn't much of a teacher, but he shared what he knew of Christianity with more than 70 people. Once, he sent across to the other side of the mountainous island for word of any missionary, but there was no news at all. The old man sat down and wept, but then he took comfort; Jesus could see him, if no-one else could.

Then in 1910, two years before his death, Samson heard news from the Christian captain of a trading ship that the S.S.E.M. had begun work on Malaita and had a school at One Pusu.

"Captain, my heart is hungry for lessons!" said the old man. "Take me to One Pusu!"

So he visited the school, and then returned to his people with a young man to help him in his pastoral work.

It was Islanders like Abel, Clement and Samson who went in among their own people with the Good News. Men like those knew the local languages or learned them quickly, and had entered into an experience of Christian living. The vital job of the missionaries was to train such men at One Pusu, strengthen and "feed" them at outlying mission centers around the islands, and keep in touch with them by means of the *Evangel* and smaller mission vessels which continuously circulated among the island outposts.

*The Mission ship, "Evangel."*

# 9

# The Evangel: A Lifeline

Not many missions have the distinction—and the headaches —of owning a ship, but in the Solomons from the beginning it was a "must." How else could people and goods be transported? There were no roads, no airplanes in those days, only impossible foot-tracks and man-powered canoes. For many years there was not even radio so the *Evangel* was the only source of news, the only steady means of communication between mission centers on the different islands in the group. It also provided the only link of fellowship for Islanders struggling to follow Christ in a hostile environment. No wonder they loved to see "ship belong God" coming in!

Mission ships have come and gone since 1913, and the role of the *Evangel* has changed with the years, but Mrs. Jessie Deck's comments still conjure up the feel of ship life in those days. Her letter from One Pusu brings home the problems and the compensations of *Evangel* life as it was for many years to come:

"The evenings here are delightful. I am sitting on the deck writing, and the stars are beautiful, and the air so fresh and sweet. On the opposite shore firesticks are moving about, showing that men are out on the reef looking for fish. Northcote is in the church nearby, enjoying a quiet evening for study; it is so seldom one can get it on board. He has had a hard day's work at the engines. We were on our way to Makira yesterday and had to come back to One Pusu, 50 miles, because one of the engines broke down, and it was not safe to go on. When we were only about two miles from One Pusu the other engine refused to work and we were facing the possibility of a night at sea, drifting anywhere! We were so thankful when after nearly an hour, it was persuaded to work properly, and Northcote emerged, hot and tired from the engine-room, saying "Don't breathe—my one hope in life is to get into One Pusu harbour—I don't care what happens tomorrow!" Engines are troublesome things. Northcote has had a great deal of hard work over these and as a rule they run very well.

"I am so enjoying being more on the ship and it *is* so interesting visiting the different schools and getting to know the people. The women always seem to appreciate having a woman to speak to them.

"I think we enjoy the evenings best of all. The teachers and a few others from the "school" we are visiting come off to the ship, and we have a meeting, mostly singing, on the after-deck. There are usually a good many of us on board, often some teachers or school boys returning, and we do have such happy times together. Then the teachers linger on after the others have gone to bed, till at last, about half past nine or ten, Northcote tells them we are so tired, we must get some sleep, and they reluctantly depart. Dear boys! One cannot help loving them, and it is a very real pleasure seeing them.

Because the ship was often the only news medium, the captain needed to be able to predict exactly where the *Evan-*

*gel* would be in six months' time. Hampered by an aging, underpowered engine, cyclonic weather and some of the most dangerous reef-ridden waters in the world, it would seem that his task was impossible; how could he hope to keep faith with dates given so far ahead? Yet he had to try, because people might travel for days to a center where the ship was due to arrive. Time and again—almost without fail—God enabled this impossible task to be achieved, and the ship would arrive exactly on schedule. Indeed, one new missionary remarked naively, "I thought the *Evangel* never had any trouble!"

At each center, two or three times a year, the *Evangel* would arrive with the visiting missionary for a day or two of meetings and discussions. The local pastor-teacher and other Christians would talk over their problems, and people would make a special trip to the coast from their bush villages. The missionary would examine candidates for baptism, taking notice of the local pastor's opinion, after which, a baptismal service might be held beside river or sea.

The *Evangel* brought medical aid, as well: "sore-leg" medicine (boracic acid), Epsom salts, aspirin, copper sulphate (to eat away the crippling tropical ulcers) and other remedies. Government medical ships were few and far between.

Running the ship was more than a full-time job. In the early days, the captain alone was responsible for safety, the welfare of the ship, the engine, the hull itself, and the running of the crew. He had no accurate maps, no indication of reefs, no navigational aids, no radio. If those at One Pusu were expecting the *Evangel*, someone might hang a hurricane lamp on a post out at the peninsula tip. Otherwise, on a clear night, the captain would sail the ship into harbor guided only by the outline of the mountains—and his own experience. At Auki the sole navigational aid was a hurricane lamp on the District Officer's veranda.

Elsewhere, with no lights at all on shore, the captain

would be up the mast in the crosstrees at night so he could better estimate the deceptive distances. Often he would pray for a flash of lightning to illuminate something strategic, such as white sea breaking on a reef. Once, when Ken Griffiths was captain, the ship had been delayed with engine trouble off the island of Guadalcanal and the weather was overcast and squally, with rain and a strong wind. At 9 pm. they arrived off Marau Sound, where outlying reefs crop up a mile offshore. There were no beacons, of course, so it seemed they would have to spend an uncomfortable and unpleasant night out at sea, but just as they reached the entrance through the reef, the full moon suddenly shone through—and the *Evangel* sailed in safely at full speed.

Those in the cabins would know nothing of this; only the men in charge would see God at work in such details. Another time, for example, the captain had the anchor chain on shore, all 120 meters of it. He wanted to mark out one length, so he put a stick through a link in the chain. As he did so he noticed a crack in that one particular link! The chain could have snapped and the ship been lost if that link hadn't been brought to his notice. No wonder they felt "looked after!"

The *Evangel's* captain often had no formal training for the task at all. He was no engineer; he simply learned on the job. There was no one to turn to for advice, no engineering supplier at hand, no stores at all to go to and buy anything forgotten or needed in a crisis, so he found the ship a great training ground for faith. As Robert McBride told a new understudy, "I never start the engine without prayer. . . ."

At Fo'ondo, on one occasion, Ken Griffiths saw a soapy mixture of oil and water oozing from the base of the engine. Sea-water had eaten a hole through half-inch-thick metal into the base of the cylinder—and to reach it he had to stretch himself flat under a metal box and poke through an opening in the outer casing.

"What can we do?" he asked Norman Deck, who was living on board at the time.

"Well, I've got some artificial dental stone," said that missionary-dentist. "That would set quicker than cement."

So in it went, and at every port Ken had to put in some more.

When they got home to One Pusu harbor, Norman Deck said, "Look, I'll put in a permanent filling!"

With the cylinder block out and on shore, he got to work, lined the cavity with dental cement, and then filled it with a whole bottle of amalgam. The job lasted the life of the engine —and the man responsible later took great delight in telling the story to an appreciative group at a dental congress!

*Edwin and Dinah with Mr. Gibbins*

# 10

# A
# Shaken
# People

Over the years, God's purposes unfolded in the Solomons, but the way forward was never easy or automatic. Each step was won by prayer through times of great testing.

The story of Edwin and Dinah was a case in point. In 1926 this Malu'u couple was called by God to leave home and go as missionary teachers to the Are Are people on the southeast coast of Malaita. They were taken there in the *Evangel* by Dr. Northcote Deck, who had found them a toe-hold at Taka Taka; and they were kept in touch by the mission ship, a life-line to many like themselves.

In 1931 they were visited by Ronald Grant, who had become their nearest missionary stationed at Wai-su-su, 15 miles away on the island of South Malaita. When he landed on the shingle beach, they shook hands eagerly.

"Wonderful to meet you!" Edwin said. "Come and see our Christian village!"

Taka Taka was a long shelving bay that opened into a valley with mountains soaring to two thousand feet on either side. Edwin and Dinah's house was up on a slight promontory, looking south down the bay—and there was the whole Christian village, the fruit of nearly six years' labor: two houses and a lean-to.

Proudly, Edwin and Dinah introduced the three members of their little flock: a single girl, with appalling ulcers, who lived in the lean-to; and a married couple who had also suffered from huge tropical ulcers. Edwin had brought them down from a mountain village. With Dinah, he had prayed constantly for their healing, and every day he had washed the ulcers with "Condy's" crystals, the accepted ulcer remedy.

The new young missionary was staggered: this pitiful little group could hardly be called a "village". That night, he and Samuel Mae'ato, his companion, talked heart to heart with Edwin and Dinah.

"We've prayed and prayed," said Edwin. "I've gone up into the hill villages time after time. The people there have come down and burned our house. They stole my knife and axe, one time, and our calicoes. They've robbed our food-gardens and slashed down our banana plants. They've done everything they can think of to make us give up and go home. But when we came with Dr. Deck that time, it wasn't he who put us here. It was God who put us here. Dinah and I will not leave this place till God tells us to go home."

The little group of four then prayed afresh, and Edwin's prayer was to be long remembered: "God, I can't do anything more to win these people. You *lembe lembe* (shake shake) so that the things that bind them are loosed."

Within a few weeks, the greatest earthquakes in living memory hit the Solomons. On the west coast of Makira, Jim Wilson was swept inshore by a great wave and, though he survived, his carrier boy was killed. At Star Harbor on Makira, at 6 a.m. on October 4, John Bee ran out of his house only to be swept inland by an enormous tidal wave, along with broken houses and church, shattered fencing and coconut palms, and his cow. Deposited on the hillside, his belongings all scattered, he had no first aid for his injured legs and no dry clothes. He lay in a small yam hut, his head pillowed on two yams, while the earthquakes continued, thankful to have escaped alive. All the heathen in that district were terrified, for their *adaros* (ancestral skulls) had been washed into the sea. These skulls were kept inside the bodies of elaborately carved wooden sharks in the special *tambu* houses, and formed the focus of all their worship.

Malaita's worst quake was yet to come. On October 10, the whole floor of One Pusu harbor rose, and soon the area was pervaded by the stench of dying, stranded fish. That same day, high up in the mountains of South Malaita island, Ronald Grant was giving medical treatment to an important chief when the earth suddenly quaked violently. Returning home, he had to travel down a river in the midst of a ravine, with massive boulders hurtling down the steep slopes on either side as the quakes continued.

Shortly afterwards, Ronald was praying with a few pastors before setting out with them on a preaching trip. The question was where to go, and there seemed no light at first, so all went off to pray individually. When they met together again, Samuel Mae'ato said: "I can only think of Edwin and Dinah." Immediately, the deadness left their prayer, and all felt certain that this was God's plan.

With a fair wind, they sailed in a small cutter northwards to Taka Taka. As they came up the bay, they could see the beach crowded with people from the bush with very little clothing but many ornaments and weapons and each man clutching a spear or bow and arrows. At the water's edge, Edwin and Dinah greeted them as they stepped on to the shingle. "God has sent you!" said Edwin, his face shining. "After all this time, many people are now ready to come into the Christian village."

Edwin and Dinah joined the visitors and they all went inland to find the people devastated by what had happened during the earthquake, and very ready to respond. From the top of a high peak they had a panoramic view across Malaita, and could see the mountains scarred with enormous landslides. Great gashes scored the sides of the ridges, and here and there were small clusters of houses, desolate and broken. At the foot of one landslide were the ruins of several houses, hurled with their occupants 1000 feet down the slope. On their way back down a wide valley to Taka Taka, they came to the house of Ahikaupaine, a cannibal who had eaten 30 or 40 people. More than anyone else, this noted headhunter was the respected leader of the whole district, a man of influence who gave lavish feasts.

Like many other local people, Ahikaupaine saw the earthquakes as a demonstration of God's great power—and now here at his door once again was Edwin, talking about the great love of God. He had a picture of a man hanging on a Cross, and Ahikaupaine came up afterwards and touched it with his finger.

"That is a picture of the Son of God," said Edwin, and told him more in his own language about God's love for him.

Ahikaupaine had something definite to say: "I'm coming to your Christian village. It's like this: before, if I said I'd kill a man, then I did it. Now that I say I am coming to live in your village, I mean it. I'm not playing. I want this Jesus."

Returning to the coast, the team found already four new houses being built in the Christian village of Taka Taka, and before they left there were 30 people where previously there had been only a tiny handful. Edwin was very firm that Christians must not attend heathen feasts nor follow other pagan customs, and several inquirers had previously left him because of this. He had a great fear of a work starting out wrong, having seen the results of this in South Malaita island. But now those "prodigal sons" returned to stay, and many others joined them to become true Christians.

Edwin and Dinah were greatly encouraged, but the brand-new Christians in their village found the new Way very hard to follow at times. Ahikaupaine was going along well until he heard of an old enemy who now wanted to live in the Christian village. When both were young and unmarried, the other man had courted Ahikaupaine's wife-to-be. This action, known as *eu lau lenikeni*, was an unforgivable insult and was always the basis for a lifelong blood-feud. Either man would kill the other on sight if they met.

When Ronald Grant next visited Taka Taka, Edwin told him: "Big trouble has come. Ahikaupaine refuses to stay here. He is going back to the heathen."

Ahikaupaine was adamant. "If this man comes and lives in this village," he said, "then I'd be a coward like a woman to stay here."

"All right," said Ronald, "you come with Edwin and Dinah and me into the church and we'll pray."

"No," he said, "I can't change my mind now. What I've said, I'll do."—and nothing would persuade him; his face was like a stone, unyielding as flint. That night, Edwin and Dinah prayed with Ronald, pleading the victory of Christ and the power of His blood on behalf of Ahikaupaine and asking God to melt his heart. Next day as he was getting ready to leave, the three asked him to come into the church with them.

"Do you belong to the Lord Jesus?" they asked.

Ahikaupaine would not answer.

"Do you?" came the question again.

"Yes."

"You think about this, then, Ahikaupaine: Jesus took all the many sins that you have committed against God—you know what they were. He was crucified for your sins so that God could forgive you. All those sins are forgotten and blotted out. God remembers them no more. And Jesus now tells you this: 'If you do not forgive the wrongs of others, then your Father in heaven will not forgive the wrongs you have done.'" (Matthew 6:15)

Ronald put his hand on Ahikaupaine's shoulder, and

prayed, "God, now melt this man's heart and put Your love in him. We thank You that Your Son died for him."

It seemed impossible, but tears began to stream down Ahikaupaine's cheeks and he started to pray, pouring out his heart to God and asking His forgiveness. The other man could come to the village and he would not leave. A day later, Ahikaupaine led Ronald by the hand to show him the beginnings of a new house. "I'm building this house for that man to come and live in our village here—right beside my own house."

In Ahikaupaine's life, the love and forgiving power of God won.

Through Edwin and Dinah, God established His Church in that whole district. Today near Taka Taka there is a thriving church of many hundreds where the holy presence of God is clearly revealed in love and power.

*Taupongi with his wife*

# 11

# Rennell
# Re-opened

In the pre-dawn gloom, the captain of the *Evangel* could hear snatches of conversation between the Malaita crew, as they looked fearfully towards the forbidding fortress-island that was looming up darkly ahead.

"I'm thinking about that time they killed three of our people here," said one. "We don't know what these Rennell-ese might do this time."

"They might not like the look of us. What do you think will happen?"

It was April, 1934, twenty-four years had passed since the three Islander missionaries left on Rennell Island had been killed. During that time when the island was closed to mission work, visits by labor recruiters, anthropologists and others had helped to break down the extreme isolation of the Rennellese; they had become more accustomed to the ways of other races, and a few had even learned a little Pidgin English. Nevertheless, the crew of the *Evangel* were glad to strengthen their hearts by praying together as the ship sailed along the coast towards Kanggava Bay.

No sooner had they anchored five hours later than a host of canoes came skimming across the glittering water. Men, women and children rushed on board the *Evangel*, and poked into every corner of the ship except the carefully locked cabins. Intensely curious, they swarmed up the rigging, investigated the engine room, stared fascinated at photographs of Rennellese taken in 1910, and made themselves very much at home. Their evident friendliness was most disarming, and with the permission of Tahua, chief at Kanggava Bay, four young men were very willing to leave their island for several months' training at One Pusu. Their names were Puia, Guisanga, Puka and Temoa.

Though strong and healthy, these isolated Polynesians had never built up an immunity to common diseases of the outside world such as colds, influenza, or malaria. Within a week, all four had severe coughs, and one became seriously ill.

"Is your 'Master on top' strong?" they asked the crew. "If we were at home, we'd ask our 'Master on top', and he would know how to make this sick man all right again."

Rising to that unmistakable challenge, the crew prayed earnestly to Christ, their "Master on top". "Your power is being questioned!" they told Him. "Make this sick man well again, for your name's sake!" That night brought a change for the better; but always, whenever Rennellese came away to One Pusu, their health became a testing-ground for faith.

At One Pusu, the four newcomers proved most intelligent and very ready to fit in. They were happy and affectionate, and so full of questions that Miss Kathy Deck took them in a class by themselves for intensive teaching. They were fascinated to work their way through the ordered lessons, tracing the story of such Bible figures as Adam and Eve, Noah, and Moses. Their teacher could scarcely keep abreast of their questions.

"This Moses on Mt. Sinai," said Puia, "did he write the

Bible? Did he write on paper? Stone would be heavy for him to carry up the mountain, wouldn't it? Did he write on sheepskin so it wouldn't break quickly? How many sheepskins did Moses carry up Mt. Sinai? Why did Adam not write the Bible? Why not Noah? Perhaps these two didn't know how to write?"

As he walked away after class, he could be heard muttering to himself: "Adam and Eve started sin; Noah started ships; Moses started writing...."

When Miss Deck came to the Ten Commandments, the very first one caused a great stir:

Puia stood up angrily: "That's what we were told would happen!" he said. "Someone who came to our island told us, 'Don't let any missionaries come to Rennell! They'll take away your own gods and give you theirs.' That is what your God says: 'Thou shalt have no other gods before Me.' We don't like that commandment!"

Their teacher wisely concluded the class for that day and next morning they all read the rest of the Commandments. All four agreed that they were good laws: "If we knew how to keep them, we would be very good," they said. The daily lessons continued, steadily, quietly.

One day, Puia said: "Is everyone at One Pusu born again?"

"I don't know", said his teacher. "I think that many are."

"We're sure they are born again," Puia said firmly. "All the men and women at One Pusu love one another very much; they're good friends with each other all the time. Our Rennell people—they fight, they kill, they steal, they hate one another."

After some months at One Pusu, all four Rennellese wanted to become Christians. However, Puia—who was the chief-elect—felt they must ask Tahua's permission before taking such a step. When the *Evangel* returned them in November that year, Chief Tahua reluctantly gave his permission, and the first Rennellese Christians began living their new way of life at home. Puia returned to One Pusu for further training, and in turn other small groups of Rennellese also left their island for several months at One Pusu.

On his return home in 1935, Puia faced a time of testing. Like the other young Christians there, he knew he must avoid food offered to the *atuas* (Rennellese gods), and keep aloof from *atua* worship. There were a number of *atuas*: lesser ones, who took a special interest in certain clans and individuals, and the supreme one, whose very name they feared to mention.

These *atuas* put many *tambus* upon the people, and to displease an *atua* meant trouble: sickness, insanity or death. Before food was eaten, the *atuas* were always thanked, and at every feast a portion was put aside for them. To rebuke, instruct or give advice, an *atua* would take possession of a man and speak through him. The Rennellese said that it was unmistakably the *atua*, and not the man, speaking at such a time. The *atuas* had their own house, and parts of other houses were sacred to them too. The whole of Rennellese life was dominated by *atua* worship.

For Puia, there came a direct confrontation as soon as he stayed away from a feast. Speaking through an *atua*-priest as medium, his former special *atua* sent for him to say: "Why have you forsaken me? You always used to talk and pray with me. Why have you stopped?"

"I have another God who has given me a Book," said Puia, showing his Bible. "My God has overcome Satan and the *atuas*," he added, and showed a picture of the Temptation.

As Puia put it, "When the *atua* talked hard, I opened my Bible and read where it says "There is *one* God," and the *atua* talked quiet. But then the *atua* said, 'In time you will get sick because *atua* has power over your life.' I showed the open Bible and read out: 'I will never leave you nor forsake you.' When the *atua* heard that, the mighty power of God hit him, and the *atua*-priest looked shamed."

Puia's Bible was then taken away and left for three days in the *atua* house for the supreme *atua* to examine it. When it was returned, Puia was told: "You pray to God—but pray to *atuas*, too." Puia, however, continued to trust the power of Jesus alone to keep him.

Then came a great feast in honor of the supreme *atua*, and Puia was commanded to attend. He came. There, gathered in silent dignity, were all the chiefs in their ceremonial garments of fine matting and saffron-colored bark, their heavily-tattooed limbs stained yellow with turmeric. Each tattoo-mark, each detail of dress, the very immobility of their faces, spoke of the awesome presence. Through a medium, the *atua* called on Puia to eat of the food but Puia refused. All looked for some signal punishment to fall on him, for never in their memory had anyone dared to "answer back" to the supreme *atua*, for all knew that those in the dim past who had done so had surely died. But there stood Puia, unharmed, and now the supreme *atua* was actually admitting that all the new teaching was true: "You go ahead, but think back and pray to us too."

It seemed as if the *atuas* wanted to keep themselves level with God, saying: "We know all about God and this teaching. It is true that God made everything. He made us, too. He did send His Son to die so that men could go to heaven, but *atuas* have power, too."

As Puia and the other Christians stood firm, the new way of life began to make an impact. The two most important chiefs on Rennell, Taupongi and Tahua, decided to visit One Pusu in 1935. They wanted to find out if the teaching there rang true, and whether One Pusu was a happy place. Taupongi, chief of Lake Te Nggano, came first, and his visit was memorable. He was a huge lion of a man, full of pride, very quick to take offense, but extremely intelligent. Within six weeks, this man in middle life had learned to read perfectly the Rennellese language which Miss Clara Waterston had reduced to writing.

Great in stature and dignity, Taupongi had a vast sense of his own importance. He considered it only fitting that he should take his meals formally with Mr. John Waite, but that missionary, a small man, had a birdlike appetite, and since Taupongi would only eat mouthful-for-mouthful, this protocol presented problems on both sides! The Rennellese chief developed a great affection for Mr. Waite, and held him in considerable respect. He had to be disillusioned on one matter, however, when the five women missionaries at One Pusu discovered that Taupongi had assumed them all to be Mr. Waite's wives!

Taupongi was tremendously impressed with the love and kindness and unity he found at One Pusu, and became deeply interested in the daily Bible lessons. However, he returned to Rennell still unwilling to commit himself to this new God, this new life.

Tahua, chief of Kanggava Bay, had learned much from Puia before he came to One Pusu. He was often deeply moved during Bible class, and wanted to be "born again," but had to talk first with his people and with Taupongi.

Late in 1935, when the *Evangel* returned Tahua to his home, Mr. Waite visited Rennell and crossed the island and the Lake to call on Taupongi, arriving at 2 a.m. He wrote:

"We wakened Taupongi, who gave me the warmest of welcomes. Taupongi made a bed of many mats near his own and made me lie down, then he took a large mat to tuck me in, head and all! I prevailed on him to leave my head free, and we settled down to sleep. But suddenly he leapt from his mats, and with the light of a fire-stick, hunted among much debris for a pillow acquired at One Pusu, now black with grease and smoke, and carefully arranged it under my head. When he lay down, I surreptitiously covered it with my handkerchief. Then one of his children cried, and he tenderly soothed it, and peace reigned again. I was just dozing when our giant again bounded up, and leaning over me, put his mouth to my ear, saying 'Tahua—is he born again?' I said, 'Tahua wants Master Jesus and prays to Him.' He then said he did not want Tahua to do anything publicly till they had conferred together, and at long last we dropped asleep till daylight."

Taupongi finally refused to make any decision, but Tahua grew increasingly responsive to the Spirit of God.

For two years the door to Rennell was wide open. Then, without warning, it slammed shut. In mid-1936, news came from the British Protectorate Government that the island must be completely cut off from all outside contact because of sickness. Visiting ships had brought common infections like influenza which were often fatal to the Rennellese. For six months the *Evangel* was not allowed to return the Rennellese trainees from One Pusu—the first time it had failed to arrive on the date set. During this time, Tahua fell ill, but before he died he let go of all prayers to his *atuas* and prayed to Jesus only. Taupongi was most displeased, holding firmly to his old reliance on the *atuas'* power. Because of the veto on outside contact, the 13 very young Christians were then left on their island alone.

Two years of silence followed.

At last, in November 1938, the *Evangel* was permitted to visit Rennell again. Hopefully, the government doctor on board would soon give the Rennellese a clean bill of health so their island could be opened again. But the shore was deserted in the gathering dusk.

"There could well have been killings," said the medical officer, glancing at the beach and the frowning cliffs. "Not a sign of life."

There was a pause, and he continued: "I hear these chiefs are very jealous."

Mr. Waite immediately thought of Taupongi, who had been so proud and touchy, "Shall I go inland tomorrow and look for Taupongi?" he asked.

The doctor thankfully agreed. Time was short, and if the

missionary could bring the Rennellese to him, so much the better.

Next day, a small group scaled the cliff and set off along a bush track. To their amazement, a large new building came into view—and suddenly out streamed a crowd of people. There in the center was Taupongi, and turning to his people, he led them all in cheers of welcome for his friend!

It was extraordinary. It was unbelievable. Mr. Waite, who knew Taupongi well, looked into his face and saw a change. He asked, "Taupongi, do you love Jesus?"

Taupongi's face beamed. "Yes," he said, "I love Jesus."

"But, Taupongi, what about all your *atuas*? Have you let them go?"

"I've let all the *atuas* go completely. Now, I have Jesus only."

The new building was the village church, where the people met twice a day. They had just been inside asking God to show His power and send His ship (the *Evangel*) to visit them again, and to bless them as they went away inland that day to preach the gospel. Other churches, they said, had sprung up elsewhere on the island.

What had changed proud Taupongi during the two years of Rennell's isolation? Temoa told the story. He was a young Christian from Kanggava, and he heard that Taupongi and his people were in great distress, troubled by evil spirits. Some, in the grip of a strength not their own, had been uncontrollable. Temoa went there concerned to help, and very simply he showed Taupongi "the new and living way" which Jesus opened to us by His blood, so that we can draw near "with our hearts sprinkled clean from an evil conscience."

Temoa had a little "wordless book," and he showed Taupongi the black page which is like man's heart full of sin. He explained its meaning, not once, but many times. Then he turned to the red page, and spoke about the blood of Jesus that can cleanse us from all sin—and he showed the white page. "I went ahead," he said. "The Holy Spirit worked, and by-and-by Taupongi took Jesus."

On April 6, 1939, the very first baptismal service was held at Rennell, and nine men were baptized in the sea before a great crowd of Rennellese. Seated among them on the sloping beach was Liesbeth Schrader, a German missionary who had taught so many at One Pusu.

"I wish you could have been present," she wrote afterwards. "My tears ran down as I saw Taupongi coming so humbly out of the water."

In that little solitary island, far away from the mainstream of world events, God showed what He could do with a tiny handful of new-fledged Christians who put their trust utterly in Him.

*Justus Ganifiri (on right)*

# 12

# Cleansing
# and
# Renewal

By 1930 Malu'u had become a sad place. The people remembered the strong, eager beginning, the years when their hearts were full of joy and many were gathered into the church. Now that early, outgoing "first love" was just a distant memory, and the Malu'u church was dry.

Alan Neil, the young missionary there, found his task heavy. The strong, proud Malu'u people seemed content with a Christian life that was full of defeat. He prayed with urgency, and began to see God in action. Within a few years, Alan saw a growing hunger and response, but knew that a far deeper work was needed.

Lying a hundred miles away at the far tip of narrow Malaita, the island of South Malaita was even more disheartening. The people there had never known a strong, joyful, clear-cut church quite obviously separate and different from the old heathen way of life. The New Way and the old ways were cloudily mixed together, and many who called themselves Christian tried to follow both Light and Darkness.

In the early days there, inefficient pastor-teachers and a mass movement meant that Christianity was merely superimposed on the old ways of life and belief. Community life was very strong in South Malaita, centered around tribal chiefs, and the people were enmeshed in heathen practices that choked their weak, tender growth as Christians. The island of several thousand people was known as "the place of heartbreak" to the missionaries.

Ronald Grant, the missionary there from 1931, came to know well the low-level Christianity that prevailed. Many of the teacher-pastors, he realized, were as stumbling in their Christian walk as those they taught. Only three or four shared his burden of concern, and these became the nucleus of a forward movement, meeting together for times of prayer. Samuel Mae'ato came from Malu'u, and the others were South Malaita men: Alexander Awalosi, Heber Houenimae and Samuel Hiruwala.

For over two years, Ronald and these few pastors taught that God will never bless the life where "unclean things" are harbored, and that animist fetishes and *tambu* groves had no place in a Christian's life. God's message was, "Touch not the unclean thing and I will receive you," for light can have no fellowship with darkness.

An important message was given in every village in South Malaita, focusing on a picture in which the Cross of Christ was seen resting on the head of a serpent. The text was: "Since the children, as he calls them, are people of flesh and blood, Jesus himself became like them and shared their human nature. He did so that through his death he might destroy the Devil, who has the power of death, and so set free those who were slaves all their lives because of their fear of death."

"By coming to earth and dying, Christ has defeated the powers of Satan," said Ronald in one of his messages. "Christ has overcome the works of darkness. He is now victorious and lives to deliver us from darkness. We can now be free. No longer do we need to fear."

In front of him sat Alexander Awalosi, drinking in the message. His eyes were being opened. He pondered over the matter for weeks, and he, together with his young wife, reached a decision and came to see Ronald.

"Do you remember our baby two years ago?" he asked.

Ronald's heart quailed. He remembered only too well: that was when Alexander had come to him about a problem. "You know that big timber rainforest between Mawa and Menehelisi? Nobody ever goes through it without a lot of people shouting in front. The women always cover up their babies with leaf-umbrellas, trusting in fetishes to give protection. Every time we go home to our village, we always cover up the babies. But I don't feel happy about it."

Ronald, who had then been only a short time in the Solomons, took the matter very lightly. "Oh," he said, "I think that, in the past, when people went through that forest, the babies felt the damp and caught a chill and died."

So, without any prayer for protection, Alexander and his wife took their baby and went home through the forest with the child uncovered. That night the baby died, with blood coming out of its ears and nose, a sign recognized by all that its death had been caused by evil spirits.

Ronald had been deeply shocked, and had since come to recognize the real power of the spirit forces involved. And now here was Alexander, raising the problem again.

"We've got another baby," he said simply. "I want to trust in God to protect it by the power of Jesus' blood poured out when He died."

His wife joined him in this, and together with Ronald they prayed, covering the baby with the protection of the blood of Jesus, so that the victorious presence of the living Lord would be with them. Then, by faith, Alexander and his wife took their child throuh the forest without any leaf-umbrella to hide it. They trusted completely in God's almighty power, and the baby lived. In doing this, they pioneered a new way for the whole Christian community in that district.

From that time onward, there was a growing response from village after village. At Kalki, one man brought out his heirloom, an ancient stone fetish, to be broken. For years the people there had relied heavily on that hidden fetish to keep away sickness and bring good luck to their food-growing, as their pastor very well knew. In other villages, the people cut down their *tambu* groves wholeheartedly, and they soon began to comment on two facts: the general health of the Christian communities had improved, and the crops from their gardens were exceptionally good.

However, throughout South Malaita the grip of evil upon individual lives was still strong. Over the years, much that was deeply grieving to God in professing Christians had been covered up. In January 1935 Ronald wrote: "At these gatherings I sometimes feel desperate. I lack the rivers of Living Water. There is blessing, yes, but I long for that irresistible dynamic. Sometimes I feel as if fettered, and have to cry, 'Oh, Lord, don't fail these people.' So many come who seem almost wistful in their desire for 'something;' others come more intelligently seeking victory and power. Many of the people are mere babes in Christ, many with much that is sinful that has to be confessed and put aside. They all need the working of the Holy Spirit in power."

Meanwhile, Alan Neil had been moved to Nongosila-Nafinua on the east coast of Malaita. In mid-1935 he was on his way back by launch after a visit to headquarters at One Pusu, chugging up the Maramasike Passage that divides South Malaita island from the mainland. Above the stretch of water-rooted mangrove trees to his right he could see Ronald Grant's house on a knoll; below, the tiny pier jutted out from the muddy shore. Alan decided to break his 100-mile journey, and call in on his brother-in-law there at Wai-su-su.

Together they visited a pastors' conference in the mountains of South Malaita. The message was on the question:

"How can God take possession of our lives by His Holy Spirit?" Afterwards, as they clambered down muddy tracks, waded through rivers and squelched home across the swampy floor of a thick dark rainforest, the two missionaries talked. To their surprise, they found they had much in common. After years in the Solomons, each had discovered that he didn't really know a dynamic answer for defeated Christians, only good advice.

During that long homeward journey they talked about their own frustrations and sense of defeat in the Christian life, their powerlessness and unbelief. Both felt compelled to spend time together to unburden themselves before God and to listen to Him. The facade of make-believe had begun to be lifted.

While they waited on God at Wai-su-su, everyday life did not come to a standstill. Big, good-humored Sardius Oge and other Nongosila men had come with Alan as crew for his launch, and they got on with the job of giving it a coat of paint and an overhaul. Each morning and evening they joined the two missionaries in talking over what God had been showing them. Others, too, came along: Jared, the cook, and Kadesh Sikihi from a nearby village. Some of these men responded with deep perception. There were interruptions: someone with yaws wanting an intravenous injection or a pastor from the mountains with problems to discuss. But no interruption cut across what God was showing them; He was in charge.

Sitting on the bark-floored veranda, they discussed the problems of the districts they both knew well. Great compassion came for the people in such need, and they wanted God to rule in the Islanders' lives. But as they talked, it became clear to them that He needed to do that very thing in a much deeper way in their own inner lives. They saw that they themselves had been ignoring the sin of their own attitudes, such as rivalry, pride in its many forms, fear and unbelief, regarding these things as unimportant and unavoid-

**107**

able. The Holy Spirit showed them clearly that these attitudes deeply grieved Him, and that Christ did have a way through—of release, of forgiveness, of victory.

It dawned on them that their own minds, independent of direction from God, ruled far too much in their day-to-day decisions and activities. This made them half-deaf to God's voice and very often He had been unable to get through to them. They began to see how much of their Christian activity was "in the flesh"—"for those who live as their human nature tells them to live, have their minds controlled by what human nature wants. Those who live as the Spirit tells them to live, have their minds controlled by what the Spirit wants" (Romans 8).

In that shabby leaf-house with two corners tied to coconut palms for support, they became aware of the holy presence of God. In His presence they found that they had to be absolutely open. There could be nothing kept hidden. They had to be transparent before each other and before God.

They began to hear the voice of Christ speaking in a way they had never experienced before, and their eyes were opened to the possibilities of a real and continuous walk in the Spirit with God. As the Spirit gave light, faith welled up, and they asked God for what He showed them, knowing that He would answer. They were given a glimpse, a vision of the church in the whole of the Solomons being revived and made strong to the glory of God. Both saw that the working of the Spirit was to be in power and demonstration; that it is the will of Jesus the King of Glory to reign in power and do great things now as in the early Church. They saw that the gifts of the Spirit (1 Cor. 12) had never been rescinded.

As each went back to the responsibilities of everyday life, he knew that they were to remain united in spirit though geographically separated. From that time on, life was never to be the same for either of them. God had taken them in hand. To them it was a new beginning, but for both to continue listening to Christ and obeying Him was essential in preparing them for all that lay ahead. They knew that there could be no compromise to walking in the light, though in time it was to be severely tested.

Meanwhile, the Spirit of God continued His quiet work among the people in the Malu'u district. They asked for a conference to be held in October 1936, with Shem Irofalu and Alan Neil as speakers; and for two months beforehand God prepared very clearly the way and the messages.

From babyhood, many of the people had become addicted to two drugs: nicotine and betelnut. In the Solomons, as soon as a child was weaned, it learned dependence upon both. A mother would often put her pipe into her baby's mouth to stop it crying, and in later life the craving had a very strong hold. In a community based on sharing, the use of these drugs led to deceit, resentment, hoarding and stealing. The Malu'u Christians had a deep sense of guilt and condemnation that they were powerless to break the grip of these cravings. Behind these two drugs were spirit forces (as mentioned in Ephesians 6:12) binding them with this addiction. Seeing this quite clearly, the leaders bound the spirit forces in the name of Jesus Christ and in the power of His victory at Calvary. Alan then spoke, with the very presence of Christ radiant upon him. Everybody knew that God was speaking to them. The message was clear and the Spirit convinced them. The church experienced an amazing and lasting release, far beyond what many thought possible, and the people thanked God for shining on them with His light, and for giving freedom and great joy.

Many years afterwards, Justus Ganifiri from Nafinua wrote about his visit to the Malu'u conference: "I saw a great moving of the Holy Spirit. . . . Alan was a man that God filled with the Holy Spirit. He knew the power of God for spiritual and practical needs.

"During my time with Alan later at Nafinua, I learned more about the secrets of power written in God's words. . . . Alan asked four of us leaders, Sardius Oge, Lucius Noi,

Amasiah Unu and myself, to have with him times of prayer and Bible study, and that was the time the Lord touched my heart. That was the time my eyes started to open to see what my life had been seeking for. This was it: the Bible is the book for life and also the book of power. I had life, but where was the power? Some had given the answer that the power was for the early days when the Church began, but not for now, and this answer discouraged my life. 'If Christians do not realize power,' I thought, 'well, the heathen have power, so it would be better to hold on to our magic to help us'. Alan in his studies helped me to see that we also can have power in Jesus over all the power of the Enemy. I saw a bit of this at that time, but not in full, because I had not yet discovered the full secret."

Among those who visited the Malu'u conference from elsewhere were Alexander Awalosi, Heber Hoeunimae and Hermon Oto, who came with Ronald Grant from South Malaita. Their faith in the presence and the power of God was tremendously strengthened by the experience in which they shared at Malu'u.

After his return to South Malaita, Ronald had a day or so of quiet, listening to God, who showed him that the way forward was to put off all unbelief and to step out in faith. Together with another young missionary, Wally Wade, he climbed the slippery mountain tracks inland to Menehelisi, a Christian village, intending to stay four days. God had other plans.

The village of 100 people was perched on a mountain saddle, high above a valley, with a distant view of the sea each side. Eastwards, beyond the coconut palms, was the "saltwater" islet of Wilante, fringed with breaking surf, and the lagoon stretching south to Ro'one village. Curving through the center of Menehelisi was a broad earth track, slippery in the rain, with a row of houses on either side. Each house was windowless and floored with earth but neatly thatched. The South Malaita people are skilled, artistic builders who decorate their front walls with intricate, beautiful weaving and knot-work.

After shaking hands with young and old, the two young men had a drink from a bamboo water-container and parked their packs in the small floored house specially built for them. That first evening they spent in prayer together, and it became clear that God was saying, "*Now* is the time to go forward". The Holy Spirit came upon them that weekend, and for three months they found themselves anchored at that center.

Menehelisi was the most unlikely place for revival. Unlike Malu'u, there was no real spiritual hunger; many of the people were hardened nominal Christians, some hiding serious sins, many were cold towards God, full of divisive bitterness. The pastor himself was very far from God, two-faced, and a constant hindrance behind the scenes.

After the meetings on the first Sunday, it was apparent that the Holy Spirit was moving among the people. A tremendous release came upon them. In the large leaf-thatched church, almost the whole company of 150 men, women and children rose to their feet and began praying, oblivious of each other. This had never happened in the Solomons before. As they did so, conviction of sin came upon them. This continued every evening for several weeks. Sometimes publicly and sometimes in private, confessions began to pour out in an endless stream. The Spirit of God continued to work in their hearts until they found relief before God in confession—often of things hidden for years. One woman confessed to serious sins committed in Queensland which had hindered her Christian experience for over 30 years.

Even the spiritual pastors, men of God from villages nearby who thought they knew the situation, were shocked. Things had been far worse than anyone had imagined. For instance, in Menehelisi, a Christian village, numerous cases of adultery were brought to light.

Heber Houenimae, who was visiting Menehelisi for that

time, wrote years afterwards of his clear memories: "When the missionary gave the messsage, it really cut like a knife. It really broke down the heart. People were convicted of sin and came looking for Jesus. Men and women wept for Jesus to save them. When they came, we had to deal with them very wisely, because they had been pure heathen (though members of a Christian village) and we had to pray with them individually many times"—to give instruction so that the Holy Spirit could lead them into truth.

Every evening the missionaries were joined in prayer with Alexander Awalosi, Heber Houenimae, Malcham Manu and Hermon Oto. They brought into the open anything that hindered love, unity, faith and the flow of the Spirit in their midst. When each had a completely clear spirit towards the others, as far as he was aware, and all were of one accord, then they began to pray. By faith they entered boldly into the presence of Christ Himself through the shedding of His blood (Hebrews 10:19-22). Then they listened and worshipped until they were lifted into the Spirit. In Christ's victorious presence they made their petitions for the following day, covering each situation as they saw it.

The result was the next day the Holy Spirit went on unimpeded with His program, working in a hundred ways of which they knew nothing. Where conviction was needed, it deepened; where illumination was necessasry, it was given. Those who were walking in the Spirit found that God was in charge; those opposing were powerless, and began to see themselves as guilty before God.

The Enemy did not give ground without a battle; there were many attempts to hinder and disrupt. For instance, every night for a whole week there was a suddening deafening downpour of torrential rain during the evening service so that people could not hear themselves talk or even pray. At last the little group of leaders prayed together to the One who stilled the storm, and no further rainstorms came to disturb the service.

Another time, the diversionary attack came through Timothy, the chief. Although Christian in name, Timothy feared that the rule of God would undermine his own power and authority. He called for a big feast, and began preparations. That night, the little group prayed that God would overrule—and soon the idea of a feast faded away for lack of interest. The people proved unwilling to co-operate. This was a humbling experience for Timothy, and for his cousin, the pastor. At last they were able to hear God's voice clearly, and real faith sprang up in them, too.

Sometimes the village people crept up to the missionaries' house to eavesdrop in the darkness. When they saw the obvious answers to prayers they had overheard, an awe came upon them. Over all the village communities in that district, God's presence was like a light shining continuously. Nothing could remain hidden in that light. Whether people were resting in their houses, working in their food-gardens, sitting in church or visiting a coastal market, that light was shining upon them inescapably. For three months this continued, and people were unable to hold out against it. If any resisted and refused to humble themselves, they became overwhelmingly distressed. Any sin which the light revealed had to be brought out into the open—and then immediately came the peace and joy of God's Spirit.

One night, Ronald Grant was wakened by someone banging on his bed.

"Come quickly! Adam Ahukela is dying!" said a village man urgently.

Ronald got up, put on his boots, and went with him to Adam's earth-floored house. By the firelight inside he could see people crowding around Adam, a tall gaunt asthmatic whose arms were held up by ropes from the rafters so that he could sit upright on his sleeping mat. He was gasping for air.

"Pray for me! I'm dying," he said, fighting for breath.

Ronald asked him, "Is anything on your mind, Adam?"

**113**

He said, "I wanted to hide this, but I must say it now. At Fairymead in Queensland I committed adultery, and I've hidden it ever since."

Within a minute, to the amazement of everyone round him, Adam was breathing normally. From that moment, his asthma began to disappear, and he came back fully into the joy of Christ.

Old Mae-hui, a stocky, bow-legged little witchdoctor, had never let the truth of Christ touch his life in the slightest. For years he had been living in the Christian village of Menehelisi, though never before sighted by a missionary. When the power of the Holy Spirit was released in that village, however, he was thoroughly stirred up. He would jump around in his house, and dance on hot coals with high-pitched cackles. The little group of missionaries and Island leaders heard him, and prayed that the light of God would shine upon him.

One day he came and asked Alexander to explain to him all about Jesus, so Alexander took him every evening and opened up to him gradually the way of salvation. Mae-hui, a notorious murderer, became deeply concerned about himself. He came to the leaders wanting to become a Christian, and poured forth in confession to God every sin imaginable: theft, sorcery, adultery, murders. They just let him go on until he had finished. When assurance came that his sins were now forgiven, his thanks poured out and his joy was unbounded. Within two hours he was standing up in front of a large crowd at a heathen feast, telling everyone how God had come into his heart.

But all his life, Mae-hui had been given over to evil spirits, and after his conversion a demon overpowered him again. It needed to be specifically dealt with. So the very next day a man came running to the missionaries, crying: "Come quick! Old Mae-hui is shaking terribly. An evil spirit has come upon him." They rushed off to his house, and found him crying out in an unearthly way. One hand was gripping the

**114**

rafter of his hut and shaking it with supernatural power. His other hand was wielding an adze.

The missionaries asked for the protection of Christ's presence to be round about them. They stepped forward, and one of them laid his hand on Mae-hui's shoulder. In the name of Jesus Christ he commanded the demon to leave the old man immediately. In his own language Mae-hui called out, "Lord Jesus, save me from this devil's power!" and the demon left him straight away. He fell to the ground in a comatose state, but in a few minutes he was himself again. Mae-hui said that when he had seen the missionaries coming, although he was overpowered by the demon at the time, he had realized inwardly, "I'm on *your* side!"

The movement of the Holy Spirit went far beyond Menehelisi to places they had not yet visited. As Heber wrote later, "The people around Menehelisi came there day after day. We did not visit every place, but we held meetings at that main center." It was as if the Spirit of God followed the visiting people back to their own villages.

At Korotalau, for instance, where fine pastors (Samuel Hiruwala and Hermon Oto) had prepared well, the spirit of prayer came down upon the people in a remarkable way. As at Menehelisi, even when ten or twenty were praying at once, they were almost oblivious of anyone but themselves and God; yet to their minds all was done "decently and in order", and the work of the Spirit continued there. All this took place without any visit by a missionary.

During this three-month time at Menehelisi, Clement Maelalo and others visited the district to see for themselves what was happening. Clement, an extremely able and spiritual man, became absolutely thrilled as he saw the power of the Spirit. He began to realize the difference between mere prayer and the prayer of faith. He went back to his own area, the Langa Langa Lagoon, to enter into the presence of Christ and pray with new-found reality. Throughout that whole district of West Kwara'ae many repented and found renewal in Christ, and God's holy presence came upon village after village.

A great beginning had been made in South Malaita in uniting missionaries and Islanders together powerfully in the Spirit, resulting in a sorely needed deep cleansing work among the people. From a human point of view, this work at that time was stopped when two of the missionaries came down with scrub typhus. The full flow of the Holy Spirit was checked for a period, but the people could never forget how the holy presence of God Himself had come into their midst. God had His own plans for the complete fulfilment of the vision He Himself had given to those involved. He had inspired in them believing prayer not only for Malu'u, East and West Kwara'ae and South Malaita, but for the whole of His Church in the Solomons.

For 30 years a great preparation was to take place. The Islanders were to attain full stature as a people, and to shoulder responsibility. Upon a Church that had come of age God planned to pour out His Spirit in even greater measure.

Many years later, after the revival in 1970, Heber Houenimae could say: "This is the second revival that I have experienced, and I thank God for it."

# 13

# Nurturing Christians

As dusk fell, a short, nuggety man was sitting on the split-palm bench in front of his house, looking out at the village of Mage where he was pastor. Smoke from the cooking-fires was filtering through the leaf-thatched roofs, and a group of youngsters suddenly dashed round a corner, shouting and laughing as they chased an old football.

John Maedola gazed after them, and again the thought came upon him strongly: there were so many young people full of energy and capacity who needed teaching—but where could they go? One Pusu couldn't care for all of them and there was nowhere else at all.

He thought about this matter of "teaching." In Island terms of those days, John himself was the village "teacher" for it was the name given to the pastor of a Christian village, who cared for his people's welfare, learning and health as best he could. He was their minister, taking the Sunday services, and their Bible teacher, giving basic literacy classes for adults and children several times a week. He was the one to whom they came for counsel and help in time of trouble. The only formal training that most pastor-teachers had was two years at One Pusu, and they taught without pay, "as unto the Lord," growing their own food-crops like everyone else.

Each morning the church-drum at Mage would call the villagers to their church for their lesson from Bible Outlines: the same lesson each day for a week. John would teach as he was taught at One Pusu, slowly but thoroughly, making sure the people understood the Bible passage and its message for daily living. Most evenings he would take the reading class on the basis of "each one teach one," when those who knew something would help those who knew less —a very noisy process! On other evenings the villagers might meet together to sing or to pray.

It was a full, busy life—yet here was this persistent thought that kept coming to his mind: the crying need for schools where young Islanders could learn. Could it be that God wanted *him* to start a local boarding school, and would such a completely new venture work out?

The strong, brooding face set with new determination as that nagging thought was replaced by peace and a sense of purpose. John Maedola was filled with a certainty that he must step forward, and that God would be with him. In 1934 he began.

Completely independent of mission support, John built his school at Mage, half an hour's walk from present-day Auki township. He cleared land and planted the necessary food-gardens with only sporadic help from the local Christians. Within a few months he had 70 pupils, most of them older boys and girls. As he said, "It is hard for me to manage the children all myself with only one helper. . . ."

Some years later, missionaries visiting the school found 143 students and 11 married couples who were responsible for food-growing and cooking. There were four pupil-teachers and five prefects to help John, but no one in the school received any pay since all their work was given as service to God. When money was neded to buy slates and books, school members would earn it by repairing Bibles and hymnbooks for the local people, or by helping to unload ships' cargo at Auki.

After the visit, Violet Sullivan wrote: "We were amazed to see all that John had accomplished with very inadequate help. The young people were clean, orderly and obedient. He kept perfect control without raising his voice. He managed to keep the many classes happily occupied, and supervised the pupil-teachers and helpers. He did not talk about himself and his doings, but he *lived* Christ and was spending himself and all that he had in God's service."

When the boys and girls first arrived, John would talk with each one individually. He wanted to find out how much or how little they knew, and he wanted some idea of where they were spiritually. Then, as a faithful "teacher," he would pray for them, keeping in close touch with those who led the Young People's Band and knew the students well. His one aim was to introduce these children to his own Master, and help them to get to know Him better. All that he taught, whether reading skills, singing or Bible classes, had that one aim in view.

John Maedola's was the first boarding school on Malaita to be established and staffed entirely by Solomon Islanders, and when others followed afterwards, they followed in his steps. It was only for eight years, however, that his school continued there at Mage. In 1942 the Solomons were engulfed by World War II, and what schools there were had to be disbanded.

---

Like the teaching of children in school, the work among women began in a special way during the 1930s. In the Solomons, the traditional culture made life for a woman extremely harsh. Yet the deep-rooted customs could not be altered overnight and it was many years before life there was transformed for women and girls in general.

One little girl, the daughter of a witchdoctor, was bitten by a snake one day, and treated by animist methods. Her people prayed to the ancestral spirits and thrust her arm into a cooking "oven" of heated stones covered with leaves. They left the child there until the arm was actually roasted, then kept her untended for ten days while they sacrificed pigs to the *akalos*. The little girl's arm was so fearfully burnt that the forearm became just a blackened, charred claw. At this stage, her people took her to the nearest missionary, Mrs. Margaret Griffiths; but by then no medical care could save the arm.

That girl victim was an example of the whole animist outlook on life, but many *tambus* and customs were biased against women specifically. In almost every case, marriage and motherhood were weighted with drudgery and unhappiness.

In the past, a marriage in the Solomons was very often arranged by the relatives who were also involved in the bride-price paid for a new wife. This exchange of island shell-money and pigs ensured a lasting contract; if the girl ran away home to her parents, they would have to return her, or else forfeit the bride-price. The husband and his relatives, on the other hand, saw to it that they got back in hard work the value of the pigs and money they had invested. The other recognized form of marriage was for a couple to run away together into the jungle and stay away several days. When they returned, they had to either pay the bride-price money to the girls' relatives or work hard for them all their lives as repayment of that debt. Marriage held little romance.

A woman was looked upon primarily as a burden-bearer. Even just before her baby was born, she had to go on working, trudging miles to the food-gardens, cutting firewood from huge logs, carrying loads of food and fire-wood that might weight 100 pounds, or hoisting on to her back several segments of bamboo filled with water for household needs. Her husband would walk with her to the food gardens, carrying his axe or knife and his weapons to defend his wife against surprise attack. He would undertake the heavy work of felling the trees to clear the ground, but he would never dream of carrying food, water or firewood; that was women's work.

Childbirth was an ordeal to be faced alone, lest the *akalos* be angered and bring sickness and death upon the tribe. During her weeks of isolation, the new mother had to live in her special hut with only a tiny fire for warmth and for cooking.

One young mother in the mountains behind Sinarango was lying asleep in her hut beside the smouldering coals when a gust of wind blew leaves into the fire, and instantly her hut caught alight. She woke to find it in flames, and crawled outside with her baby before rushing back to grab her mat of sewn pandanus leaf. (Smoke from the mat would anger the *akalos* and bring retribution on her family, because the mat was *tambu*: she had lain on it after her confinement.)

While saving the mat, her back and legs were extensively burnt, especially behind the knees. She lay outside with her newborn baby in the dew and cold mountain air. Several days later her burns were all festering, and both mother and child were suffering from cold and shock. News came to the husband, who was troubled about his wife because she had been a good worker, efficient and obedient. He was looking after the two older children and the pigs.

"No matter," said his father. "Let her die. She is only a woman. I am a rich man. I will give you many strings of money to buy another wife."

However, the husband was not satisfied since he thought she was worth saving, if possible. From his relatives' point of view, of course, nothing could be done because she was untouchable, *tambu*. But the husband remembered the

Christians down by the sea who were kind to sick people and not afraid to touch a woman after a baby's birth. So he went down to the Christian village and asked Elisha Sareto'ona, the pastor, for help.

"Will you Christians go up and carry my wife down to your village and look after her?" he said.

Elisha said, "Suppose we do that, and she gets better, by and by you'll take her back to the heathen again. We want this woman to get life. We are willing to do this hard thing so that she can get life, so that we can teach her about God."

The husband agreed to this, but Elisha said: "I think you're just pretending. By and by you'll want to take her back."

"No, I'm not pretending," said the husband. "I'm talking true."

With some girls to help him, Elisha then went up the mountains to help the woman. They made a stretcher of saplings and bark, and covered their patient with large leaves before carrying her and the tiny baby down the steep tracks to the village.

Then Elisha set off by canoe to Nongosila to ask Joan Deck for advice and help. When he told of burns on the woman's whole back and side, right down her leg, Joan was aghast. "I haven't even enough bandages to cover that area!" she said. All she could give him was sterilized vaseline and an empty kerosene tin. Elisha was glad of this tin to carry water from the river and heat it on the fire, and the girls carefully washed the woman all over.

Elisha decided to use the leaf of a *finu finu* tree to make an island medicine. Leaves were gathered and burnt to ashes, and the ashes mixed to a paste with which the extensive burns were covered, excluding the air. Every second day, the girls washed off the ash dressing and put on a fresh one, and slowly the woman recovered.

Later, Joan came by canoe to see how they were getting on, and she never forgot the girls' shining faces as they showed

**122**

her their patient with great joy. Every day they had been teaching her about the Lord Jesus who loved her.

Elisha had partitioned off part of his leaf-house for the sick mother, and Joan went in to see her. There she lay, beautifully clean, and with her skin mostly healed over. She had a look of great peace on her face, and Joan knew she had passed from death to life.

"What has happened about the baby?" Joan asked Elisha.

He said, "My wife, Charity, has a small baby, so she feeds the new one, too."

Remembering how an Island woman sleeps on a mat with her baby beside her, Joan asked where the little one slept.

"I myself take the little stranger baby to keep it warm at night," he said.

About a year later, Joan visited the Christian village again, and saw the woman still living there though her husband had come down with many strings of money to get his wife back.

"Do you think we did this hard thing for money?" Elisha had asked. "What's money? In no time it is gone. We did this so that your wife would get life. She belongs to God now, and we want her to stay here. We want you and your children to come down to live with us and learn about God who is stronger than your *akalos* and wants you to trust in Him."

So the husband had brought his two children down to the coast, and Joan saw him and his family outside a leaf house built for them by the little Christian community.

The messasge of love and freedom from fear brought many into the Kingdom. Among the Christians, no woman was forced to be alone during childbirth, and the *tambus* that weighed down her life were broken. The new outlook brought new customs of care for the sick and concern for others, and gradually the people learned too, how to build healthier homes, with floors and separate kitchens. To bring Christian teaching to the women and girls, however, was a difficult task; their lives were so full of drudgery, and their horizons so limited.

Concerned to meet this need, Violet Sullivan in 1937 started a Women's Band at One Pusu for the wives of married students. Timothy Anilafa's wife, Elizabeth, became the leader. A wise, humble woman, very intelligent and capable, her husband found in her a quiet, strong influence for good. He used to say of her, "United we stand, divided I fall!"

In the midst of caring for her eight children, Elizabeth gave warm friendship to the wives from many language groups who came to One Pusu. Each week, a dozen or more would gather together for Women's Band, and Elizabeth encouraged all to take an active part. The women themselves would help to give the messsage, read from the Bible, choose a hymn, or pray. Those with young children learned how to tell them simple Bible Stories in the regular Mothers' Story Class.

At Fo'ondo in North Malaita this new idea of Women's Band took root and became established. Margaret Griffiths found herself tied at home there by her young baby, unable to go out into the villages much. With a handful of women, she started a time of sharing their concerns each week. Together they formed a Women's Band at Fo'ondo, and before long 100 women from many villages were coming each Sunday.

The women would walk for hours to attend their special meeting and take an active part, and the old women especially loved being included. Their Band became much more than an ordinary "women's meeting;" it proved to be the seed of a "grassroots Christianity" that spread into the homes and lives of countless families.

In the villages, most women could not read and so could not feed themselves on Scripture at all; alone, they could only pray. But when they were taken individually and patiently taught one simple verse and its meaning, they were pathetically grateful. One woman said, "I don't just think about that verse in my prayer-time. I think about it all day while I work in the food-garden."

The nucleus of Fo'ondo women—Claudia, Peace, Kaziah, Beulah and Grace—soon found to their delight the value of "one by one" work. As they began visiting a nearby village noted for its quarrels and angry shouting, they found the poor old women there could hardly read. They were so grateful and responsive and glad to be fed with spiritual food that the whole tone of the village completely changed.

To "feed" such women unable to read, Margaret suggested giving them just part of one verse, in their own language, over and over until the knew it by heart and it became food for thought for the following week. Those who wanted something to do for their Master could then teach that verse to someone else in their home village. In this way, many of the rank and file began to realize to their great joy that they, too, had a job to do, even though they might not be able to learn to read and were too old for formal schooling. Before this new approach, they had thought that only the teacher-pastor could do God's work.

Little children too, had been neglected—simply from ignorance. Their mothers did not know how to teach them and left it entirely to the village pastor. They were thrilled to discover how responsive a little child can be, and were most interested in learning how to tell Bible stories, ask questions, and teach their little ones how to pray.

Nearly 40 years after that small beginning at Fo'ondo, Olive and David Daifa wrote: "We had great joy and blessing when we saw this work of Women's Band that God used Mrs. Griffiths to start years ago in North Malaita. God is working mightily and using the women to stand on their own feet to carry out what God wants them to do." For the married women and the old folk, the Women's Bands that took shape in the 1930s opened up unthought-of possibilities. For the young girls of the Islands, more sustained teaching was practicable; life for them was just beginning, and their minds were still open and receptive.

Late in 1934, a group of shy, excited girls clambered from the *Evangel's* dinghy on to a short stone pier. They were the very first arrivals at Afio Girls' School, and there to meet them were Joan Deck and Molly Jenkins.

"How good to see you all!" Joan said, greeting those she knew by name. "Come along this way, everyone! Come and see your new home."

Each with her small parcel of possessions, the girls followed Joan and Molly up the steep hillside. The track was a swathe through the dense, wet jungle, with timber-edged steps cut into the sharply rising ground. At the top, their climb ended on Joan's wide veranda, and the girls gazed admiringly at her house. It was leaf-walled like their own, but it had a raised floor and a roof of galvanized iron to catch rainwater in a tank. No need to climb up from the stream with heavy bamboos of water, here!

"Now you look out this way," said Joan, pointing southeast. "Anyone from Makira? You can see it, and Guadalcanal, to, from here. Any time you are homesick, you can look across the sea to your own island. And you girls from Big Malaita, you can just look up this way, across the Maramasike Passage."

Perched healthily on a high point of land near the South Malaita coast, Afio School was ideally situated. It was easily reached from all three islands, and in those days suitably isolated. Parents felt that their girls were safe from intruders, and readily sent their daughters there for two years' training.

Joan took the new arrivals along to show them where they would be living. All the buildings were grouped round a central knoll that in time would be covered with brilliant green Japanese clover. Across the slippery red clay soil were paths of gleaming white coral fragments, with deep drains each side to catch the heavy rainfall. Despite its poor soil, Afio was to become like a botanic garden, with vivid hibiscuses,

**126**

graceful shrubs and Honolulu shower trees against a back-ground of tall-timbered rain forest. Past the small hospital ward, the girls came to a large dormitory-cum-classroom, floored with beautifully laid hardwood. At the end of the room were racks for their bedrolls and a half-kerosone-tin each for storing personal belongings. By day, classes would be held here; and at night, all the wooden benches and desks would be pushed aside to make room for 40 girls on sleeping mats.

The next building was a sizeable church, and down the slope behind the dormitory were the kitchens. Joan took the girls inside one.

"Is this like home?" she asked, and the girls gazed around them. With the knowledge born of years sharing village life, Joan had created for her students an exact replica of their own style of kitchen, thatched with leaf and floored with earth. There were the stones for building an island-oven, and the neat piles of broad leaves for wrapping food. Above were the racks of firewood and the cooking bowls. Joan well knew how important it was for her Afio girls to fit back easily into village life again, after training. All their food would be cooked in island style, and each day the girls would work hard in the food-gardens, growing fanna, yams, taro and sweet potatoes, as they would at home. From the beginning, there were five married couples assisting at Afio. The men would cut down the enormous trees of the virgin forest to clear the ground, and their wives would help look after the girls and supervise their work in food-growing.

At first, the new students were so nervous that they seemed incapable of answering questions or "telling back" a story, and they never had the courage to ask their own questions. Their lives had been so limited, so full of drudg-ery, that their mental capacities had never been developed. In time, Joan grew to realize their potential, and to love teaching them. She gave them a simple but varied diet in their schooling: geography lessons, with volcano-shapes built in sand, and a weathercock to help teach compass directions; conversation in English, not Pidgin; simple arithmetic; and singing, which they loved. At first, all the Bible lesson notes were written out on the blackboard, but later some of the girls when taking meetings wrote their own notes and even learned to conduct church services.

On Saturday evening, the cleared dormitory made a wonderful place for games and singing together. At home, a girl never had much fun or time for games; there was always work to be done—minding younger children, cooking, food-growing, carrying water. At Afio, Joan taught them how to sing in rounds, which they loved, and how to play games like Musical Chairs and Hunt the Thimble. Before the final prayer on Saturday night, there was always a relaxed time for sharing news from everywhere, and for talking.

In those first years at Afio, the girls came very young and completely unschooled. They were shy and often unpromising, with a very limited outlook on life and no knowledge at all of reading or writing. The teaching then had to be in Pidgin English, and there was a strong emphasis on Bible teaching and counselling to fit the girls for Christian work in their own villages afterwards. Many proved themselves staunch Christians, as wives and mothers at home after their Afio training. They helped the sick, taught Sunday School and Bible classes, and shared with the older women, especially through the Women's Bands.

This new emphasis on training the Island women and giving them spiritual food, both at Afio and through Women's Bands, proved its worth in the war years. When World War II hit the Solomons in 1942, the Girls' Bible School of course had to be temporarily disbanded; but in the villages it was mostly the women who held the people together under Christian influence, carrying on with services while their men were away involved in war work.

128

# 14

"Thus
Far and
No
Further"

In December 1941 "Pearl Harbor" hit the headlines of the world, and a flood of Japanese poured over the areas southeast of Asia for half a year. In May 1942 they occupied Tulagi and Guadalcanal in the Solomons, and that lonely corner of the Pacific exploded into one of the world's major battlegrounds.

For those caught in the crossfire, events moved swiftly after Pearl Harbor. Early in 1942, most missionaries and other Europeans were sent home, and only a few Government officials, coastwatchers and others were allowed to remain. At four S.S.E.M. centers a handful of missionaries (John Waite, Norman Deck, Bob Vance, Wilbur Clark and John Hobern) stayed on to stand with the people during this time of dislocation and danger, but all three training schools had to be disbanded.

As the danger of invasion increased, the Government advised people to leave their villages and hide in the jungle. The normal routines collapsed, and there could be no more regular teaching of basic literacy and Bible classes; only the daily services continued, where possible. With the slackening of Government control, some found it tempting and easy to loot; and with the breakdown of church and village life, some forgot about God and returned to the old ways. Those who lived to please their Master and those who were unchanged in heart followed diverging paths under the stress of war.

Tension increased with the Japanese successes in May. Until that time, the administrative capital of the Solomons had been Tulagi, on Nggela Island midway between Guadalcanal and Malaita, but this strategic prize was taken by the invaders. Soon the Japanese were well entrenched on Guadalcanal, too, developing an air base that is now Henderson Airfield near Honiara. Powerless, humanly speaking, the people of the Solomons waited in the shadow of disaster.

Invasion threatened Malaita, and One Pusu in particular, with its airfield potential and its fine harbor. Mr. Waite, John Hobern and the five young Islanders still there at the S.S.E.M. headquarters were well aware of the danger, but they had no clue that on August 6 a big Japanese ship was heading for Malaita.

August 7, 1942: It was breakfast-time at One Pusu, and American planes were zooming overhead! The Allies had arrived, and the invaders' ship, held overnight on a sunken reef, had been bombed. But One Pusu needed protection from friend as well as foe, as events soon proved. At midday, U.S. planes bombed the mission launch in the harbor there, having heard that Malaita was Japanese-occupied and inhabited solely by wild natives.

The U.S. aircraft-carrier was anchored at Taka Taka on the east coast, and Timaeus Teioli, a young Government headman, heard of it. It was his job to report any ship's arrival, and to see if it were friend or enemy. Wearing an old loincloth instead of his uniform, he cautiously approached by canoe. The Americans were very wary, thinking he must

**130**

be a spy for the Japanese whom they firmly believed were occupying Malaita. They frankly disbelieved him when he said that the island was not yet occupied.

"Nonsense!" they said. "We've just been over one big station on the west coast. It's a place with many buildings on a point. We've already bombed a Jap ship there, and tomorrow we're going to bomb the whole place to pieces."

Timaeus was appalled, since he knew of course that it was One Pusu. "Don't bomb there!" he begged. "That's my station where I learned to read. Two of my missionaries are there!"

"You can read?" they asked, and gave him a U.S. coin. "Here, you read this."

He turned the coin over in his hand, and read aloud, "In God we trust." To the American officers he said, "We trust Him. He is our God. The missionaries have taught us to love and serve Him." Then he read from a Bible they found for him, with obvious familiarity.

On a chart Timaeus showed the location of each missionary and each Government official. Instead of bombs, the Resident Commissioner received a little visiting card— "with the compliments of the Commanding Officer!"

The Americans had come in to retake Guadalcanal and Tulagi, but their arrival that day in August checked the Japanese advance on the very threshold of S.S.E.M. territory, the heavily populated island of Malaita. It was as if the One to whom all authority in heaven and on earth is given had said: "Thus far, and no further."

The Japanese fought bitterly to retake Guadalcanal, and months of fierce fighting on land, sea and air enveloped the island. The local people were asked if they could like to help the Americans by providing labor, and many young men entered the Labor Corps to work on Guadalcanal and at Tulagi. One of these was Jesimiel Maenuta, who became a sergeant over 24 men. Together they carried cargo: ammunition, food, steel matting for airstrips. As Jesimiel remembers, "At that time we could never sleep properly because the Japs bombed Tulagi every night. We had to stay in foxholes till early morning, and sometimes the holes filled up with rain. Every night without fail at 7 p.m. the bombing would start.

"There were many Christians among us, and we didn't have any time or place where we could have prayer. So some of us asked our captain if we could build a church-house, and he agreed. We had a service after each day's work, and the American chaplain used to take the Lord's Supper for us."

On Guadalcanal, Jacob Vouza distinguished himself by exceptional bravery. Captured by the Japanese, he was tied to a tree and tortured in order to force him to betray the U.S. positions. He refused, was bayoneted, and left for dead. He revived, managed to free himself from his bonds with his teeth, and crawled to the American lines, where he insisted on giving his report before accepting any medical help. He was later awarded the Silver Star and the George Medal.

Whether by bravery (like Vouza), by kindness, by hard work, or by gleaning information, the people of the Solomons proved themselves staunch friends to the Allied forces. Their warm welcome often came as a shock of surprise to airmen expecting to encounter fierce tribesmen when they crash-landed.

Beneath a vine-hung banyan tree on the east coast of Malaita, an American pilot crouched exhausted on a late December day. In the night he had ditched his plane and been washed ashore on an island that was unknown to him. He smeared his badly scratched face and hands with thick mud, and found a hidingplace. For all he knew, the country was enemy-controlled. But as daylight came, he heard men's voices speaking a foreign tongue, so he cocked his gun and lay hidden, wedged between the massive tree-roots, waiting. He could see a group of Islanders on the beach with their canoes, but suddenly one of them left the group and came straight towards the banyan tree, slashing vines with his long knife.

"S-s-s-s!"

The Islander jumped, startled at the sound, and found himself gazing into the muzzle of a gun. But the eyes that met his were not those of a Japanese; they were blue. Bili knew he had nothing to fear.

"Friendly?" said the American, still covering Bili with his gun.

"Yes."

"Friendly America?"

"Yes, friendly America."

At that, the airman clambered stiffly out from his hiding place and ordered Bili to lead the way to the other fishermen. His gun was still in his hands, ready.

Reassured by the answers to his questions, the American gained confidence that he was in friendly hands. Gingerly, he balanced himself in one of the canoes, seated carefully in the middle, while his new friends pushed off and paddled for home—the tiny reef-surrounded islets of Nongosila, 12 miles to the south.

Sardius Oge, a leading man on the island, gave the stranger a warm welcome; and all the people crowded round to shake hands with the man they called "Mr. America." They bathed his lacerated face and hands, using their small store of iodine, and the women prepared a good meal of fish and sweet potato. Then Sardius took the airman to his own house to sleep. Before they left him, Sardius gave simple thanks to God for sparing the airman's life and letting them find him.

After a good night's sleep, the airman was taken up-river to Nafinua, the nearby mission center. There among the crowd on the stone jetty were three white men: Norman Deck, Bob Vance and Wilbur Clark. "Mr. America" introduced himself as Lieutenant Polk, a newspaper man in civil life, very glad indeed to spend Christmas with them, and five quiet days. He liked to wander into the village and chat with

**133**

Justus Ganifiri, whom he greatly appreciated; and on Sunday he joined the big crowd in the village church.

Picked up soon afterwards by a seaplane in response to his signals, Lieutenant Polk returned to drop from the skies a surprise package. Inside were medicines, candy, magazines and—praise God!—boots for each of the missionaries in exactly the right sizes. The thoughtful visitor had quietly noted their needs and unknowingly answered special prayers.

"God still has His ravens," said the Islanders, remembering the story of Elijah, "but another kind this time!"

During 1943, the center of conflict moved away from the Eastern Solomons, but the involvement with war continued. Young Solomon Islanders worked with Americans at the U.S. base on Guadalcanal, and one of them was Jeriel Gapu, aged 16. His impressions show the impact that war made upon Island minds.

He saw the cost of war in human life: "At Lunga Beach, we stayed beside the big U.S. cemetery. There was a building always filled with dead people, and every day men were buried."

He worked with cargo for a year, and saw quantities of goods unimagined before: cargo tall enough for a man to stand on and pick a coconut from a lofty palm! There were foodstuffs and ammunition, rifles and iron tanks. And then he saw the wastage of war—surplus goods discarded, to his astonishment. As war came to an end, new cars, jeeps, trucks and even airplanes were deliberately destroyed by the authorities. Unwanted machinery was loaded on to large pontoons, each with a bulldozer in the middle to push everything overboard into the sea. Perfectly good cans of food were smashed up and buried so as to leave the Island economy a little nearer its state before the war. But to Solomon Islanders' eyes, it made no sense.

World War II changed the center of gravity in the Solomons. Until that time, the government base had been Tulagi, on the thinly populated island of Nggela. It was bombed out of existence during the fighting, and lost all importance. In its place, Honiara on Guadalcanal became the growing point. The peaceful coconut plantation there had been transformed into a strategic air base, with Henderson Airfield nearby. After the war, it developed into a busy township which is now the capital of the Solomons.

War in the Pacific came and went, but the Solomons could never be the same again. The even flow of life had been disrupted. The broken routine of village teaching could not be restored for several years after the war, and this gap in foundational teaching affected a whole generation of children. New ideas had arrived with the Americans, and the Islanders talked with many, among them some who had skins as dark as their own. The whole experience of war was education in a hard school for the Island people, and out of it came new movements such as "Marching Rule" which changed the course of future development.

The war and its aftermath closed a chapter in the Solomons. During the 36 years there since 1904, the missionaries of the S.S.E.M. had been inevitably affected by the paternalistic outlook of their own generation towards Solomon Islanders. After the war there was to come a gradual but dramatic change that ultimately broke down social barriers between the Islanders and the white people who lived in their country.

# 15

# Marching Rule and God's Overrule

In March 1950, Arnon Atomea was in jail at Gizo, 200 miles from his home island of Malaita.

"I could hear the roosters calling for the sun to come up," he remembers. "I could see a man standing there at the foot of my bed, but I couldn't look at him. He was too shining. He said, 'On May 5, at 12 o'clock, you will get free.' "

And so it happened: at noon on May 5, Arnon and the other eight chiefs of the Marching Rule movement were released, more than two years before their six-year sentence expired.

Arnon was not the only devoted Christian to find himself in jail when the Marching Rule movement swept like wildfire through Malaita after World War II. It had seemed so good to start with, and its real name, *Ma'asina Ruru* in the Are Are language, means "brotherhood together." There was no hint then, of future trouble.

It was Alick Nono'ohimae, an Are Are man, who called the first meetings in 1943, and the aim of *Ma'asina Ruru* was clear—Malaita people must work together to achieve specific goals. Its members wanted a paramount chief, heading a committee, to represent all Malaita. He would be able to negotiate fairer wages for plantation workers, and insist that Malaita's tax be used to develop Malaita. They also wanted an effective educational system and Solomon Island magistrates who could understand traditional "custom" law. *Ma'asina Ruru* called for a High Commissioner who actually lived in the Solomons and for community development through co-operatives.

Soon the ideas of *Ma'asina Ruru* began to spread throughout Malaita, and each tribal division chose its own chief from the local line of chiefs. Nine chiefs were elected, and other leaders chosen to work under them.

At that stage, Marching Rule had no quarrel with Government, mission or medical workers, and it won respect from missionaries and government officials. Progress was steady—but for some it was far too gradual.

"The Are Are way is too slow!" said one group impatiently. "We'll be dead before we get all we want! Look—we've got our own chief now, and we've got our own reformed 'custom' laws and our clerks. Why do we need the Government courts and laws at all? We can set up our own courts!"

Some were cautious and tried to give warning: over-hasty action could bring conflict. But the momentum was too strong, and no one could put on the brakes. The impatient ones took the law into their own hands, and soon Marching Rule members were holding their own independent courts with "Native Custom Duty" men as policemen to arrest wrongdoers.

This was the point where many consider that error came into the movement, since there cannot be two governments running one country. They argue that Marching Rule members acted so quickly that they jumped ahead of wise advice and without permission took the right to run their own courts.

In North Malaita particularly, village headmen appointed by the Government saw others taking over their role. They hurried to arrest those responsible for the illegal courts, and made an indignant complaint to the Government about Marching Rule people who refused to pay tax to the Government and insisted that it should go instead to their elected local chief.

In 1947 the Government took action: Marching Rule was declared an "unlawful society" movement, and its nine chiefs were sent to the distant jail at Gizo in the Western Solomons. Reaction was swift and strong. Malaita people felt that the Government in punishing their chosen chiefs, was insulting and hurting thousands of people. Identifying with their chosen representatives, they went to prison by the thousand as an act of protest. This marked the beginning of a strong feeling of national identity on that island.

Before going to jail, the chiefs had emphatically warned their people not to destroy anyone's life. Not only might the nine chiefs be killed in revenge, but bloodshed could result in civil war. Frightened and suspicious, the Marching Rule people felt a strong sense of persecution.They were prepared to die for their cause, and some even readied their machine guns for action. But the action they took instead was that of passive non-cooperation; they refused to pay taxes except to their own elected chiefs, and were therefore put in prison for limited periods.

Even the few who would not join the widespread popular movement tasted persecution. They heard the Marching Rule people say, "We'll put them on another island, if Marching Rule wins!" In the close-knit community life, it hurt to be snubbed as a small minority group that refused to join in with fellow-Islanders.

Once the nine chiefs were in jail, the state of Marching Rule varied widely from district to district. Among the Are Are people, very few were put in prison because the local Government headmen were on the side of Marching Rule there. Agricultural co-operatives were begun, and stringent rules against stealing were strictly obeyed.

In other districts, however, the movement acquired new aims and a new emphasis on "cargo cult" ideas. "We don't need the Government!" people said, "We have our own now. As long as the British Government is here; there's no room for others like the Americans to help us. We believe America's going to send us cargo, and we've got to be ready for it. The Government is deceiving us! And we can't trust the missionaries, either, because they're on the same side as the Government."

Antagonism was widespread, and both missionaries and Islanders were praying that the other side would change their attitude. Though it seemed impossible, God was to answer the prayers of both sides.

By 1950 the Marching Rule people still refused to give in and pay tax. They felt that if they did, the whole idea of Marching Rule, the good as well as the bad, would collapse with nothing to show for it. They were determined to have their nine chiefs released from that distant jail, and they insisted on the principle of having locally-elected Malaita chiefs instead of just Government-appointed village headmen.

At this point of stalemate, a Government representative Mr. Gregory-Smith was sent specially from England to investigate the complex situation. On Malaita, he promised the Marching Rule people that they could have their chiefs back, and all their desires worked out *through* the Government at Honiara.

Early in May, he walked into the Gizo jail and talked for two days with the nine chiefs, who were much impressed with his wisdom and with his quick grasp of their aims and viewpoints. He finally convinced them that they could trust what he said.

"You'll be released very soon," he told them, "though your sentences have not yet expired. I'd like you to go back home, tell the people that you are their leaders, collect their taxes and bring them to your own new council that you will now have."

The deadlock was broken and both sides could move forward together. That initial advisory Malaita council later became the Malaita Council, and many of the original aims of Marching Rule have been achieved in the years that have followed.

Obviously, Marching Rule greatly affected the re-establishment of mission work after the war. By 1947 most missionaries had returned but were baffled and frustrated by the changed attitudes of most people on Malaita and their unwillingness to co-operate. However, in 1951 the S.S.E.M. Directors sent to the Solomons an experienced former missionary, Rev. William Gibbins, specifically to help organize the indigenous church. With Timothy Anilafa, the most senior Christian leader, he visited all the districts and was able to form local Associations of churches. (An Association consists of perhaps 20 churches in one district, generally linked together by a common language.) Mr. Gibbins proved to be God's instrument for that job at that time.

Summing up the impact of Marching Rule, one Islander put it this way: "When we look back to those days, we see the hand of God leading, guiding and protecting—even though we didn't know it at the time. I think it was good, because otherwise we would still be as we were before, remaining undeveloped. And it's the same with regard to the Church. After we got through Marching Rule, the Associations came in, they have continued to develop until today. It was all part of the process of strengthening.

"At the time, there seemed to be no way out of the troubled situation, but—praise God—He brought us out!"

Those who were most ardently involved in Marching Rule and those who were most strongly opposed to certain aspects that developed in the movement are today bonded closely together in Christian fellowship.

*Island children*

# 16

# God's Hand on Schooling

For John Maedola, the war and Marching Rule had come like a blight upon his growing school at Mage. In 1942 he had to send all his eager young pupils home to their villages while Malaita tensed under the shadow of war. Then came the long sad years after the outward fighting was over and John tasted a new kind of conflict. Deeply loyal to his Master and to all fellow-Christians, he found that most of his friends were strongly committed to Marching Rule, yet he himself did not feel happy about joining the movement.

After those first eight years of new growth in John's school at Mage (1934 to 1942), there came eight years of total lack of educational opportunity. For Malaita people, no kind of teaching could begin anywhere until the early 1950s, when the issues and unrest of Marching Rule were resolved. The man who longed to teach had to bide his time.

The right moment for John arrived in 1951. With his close friend, Timothy Anilafa, and two other experienced senior pastors, Heman Ioi and David Irofanua, he made a launch trip to key villages of North Malaita. Their visit became an opportunity for true reconciliation among the people. God's time was ripe for a fresh start.

Within a few months, John Maedola was teaching school once more—this time, at Su'u. Years before, the mission had leased 1000 acres of rain forest 15 miles north-west up the coast from One Pusu. This gave them a site for a boarding school where plenty of food could be grown. During the war years and afterwards, missionaries had built a classroom, a kitchen, a dormitory, and a solid, roomy house. All they needed were some students willing to come and be taught, but Malaita people kept away because of Marching Rule. In 1950 the school opened with ten young men from other islands—Guadalcanal and Makira.

Within a year, numbers had doubled and Malaita people were ready to co-operate. Once more, their young men came for two years' Bible training—this time at Su'u as well as at One Pusu. The old center was no longer suitable for large numbers of students since it had no food-garden land nearby, and the cost of imported food had soared. At the new Su'u school, however, food was no problem; the river flats could support ample crops of yam and sweet potato, coconuts, paw-paws, arrowroot and bananas.

Through the middle of the Su'u property runs the Kwari-akwa River, a swift-flowing clear stream with many popular swimming holes, and the flat land beside it provides space for food-gardens and playing-fields where the boys enjoy football and athletics. Rising sharply above the riverside greenery is the bumpy hill-top where the school is built, with dormitories, classrooms, church and staff houses scattered over the cleared grassy area fringed by bush. The views from the knoll are breathtaking: the palm-fringed coastline and ever-changing sea, the river valley, or the inland hills and mountains rising in layers, jungle-clad.

To begin with, the teaching at Su'u ran parallel to the well-tried One Pusu course, and at both centers young men learned basic literacy which made the study of Scripture possible. John Maedola, the wise teacher, was like a father to

**144**

all the Su'u students and poured out wholeheartedly his last two years of life. He was adept in getting work done in a happy spirit, and had his own methods of managing men. Like the Apostle Paul, he knew the value of genuine praise, and slipped it in with affectionate joking.

"Ey, Peter-belong-me!" he would say to a student, "Here's a job for you! No one can chop logs like our Peter. Remember the time when the axe-head flew off?"

There was much hard, slogging work to establish the food-gardens, but John always made it sound as if he had a special reason for selecting each man for a specific job. In the classroom, too, and in the church services, his words went home with effect.

"Think about this," he said one day, his keen, kindly eyes scanning the young faces in front of him. "How do you *prepare* to meet God? When we go to the food-gardens, we have to prepare. You get your basket, your knife, your firestick, and your shell knife for cutting taro. And when you go by sea, you prepare the canoe. You put in paddles and a dipper, and food and drink. It's no use thinking about green-coconut juice when you're already out at sea; you have to prepare in advance.

"When we are not thinking about it, and perhaps not prepared, that is the time God will meet us. One man I knew climbed a coconut tree to the very top. When he put out his hand to grab a branch, he missed it and fell to the ground far below. God met him on that tree. He might have been ready to meet God, or he might not. Another man set out to walk to Fauambu hospital. He was not sick and no one killed him, but he fell dead suddenly on the road. God met him on that track. My sister's child went out in a canoe. A big sea came up, the canoe capsized, and the child was drowned. That girl met God on the sea.

"How can you get ready to meet God? First, you must be born again. Then, if you have new life but there is still some sin in your life, you must bring that sin to Jesus and He will cleanse you in His precious blood. Thirdly, you must get ready to meet God by doing the work He wants you to do for Him, so that you won't be ashamed when Jesus comes to take you home.

"We never know when we may suddenly have to meet our Master. One day when I was working in my food-garden, my body was very dirty and I was covered in sweat. I set out for home, not thinking specially about anything. I thought, 'When I reach the river near home, I'll have a good wash and change my laplap.'

"Then coming towards me I saw a soldier. I thought, 'He's on a job for the government.'

"As he reached me, he said, 'The government official wants to speak with you. Come right away!'

" 'I can't meet him like this!' I said. 'I'm so dirty—I'm not ready!'

" 'Doesn't matter,' said the soldier. 'You've got to come now.'

"So I had to go—and I said to the government official, 'Excuse me, sir, for not being prepared to meet you. I'm very dirty and I'm very sorry.'

" 'It can't be helped,' he replied. 'I want to talk with you now.'

"That was true enough, but how ashamed I was to be so dirty and not at all ready to meet him!

"Our Master wants us to be ready any time—like Enoch. Remember how Enoch walked with God and talked with Him all the time? When God said to him, 'Enoch, I want you to come now and I'll talk with you,' Enoch was not ashamed. He didn't have to think up any excuse. He was ready to meet God. Are you?"

John Maedola himself was called by his beloved Master in 1953. "I can see Jesus waiting for me now", he said, and his years of work on earth were ended. The teacher had gone, but the teaching continued. Others took his place at Su'u, and the Bible School there continued to grow in numbers until by 1960 there were about 100 young men in training.

Between 1950 and 1960, the Bible teaching methods that John knew so well continued at Su'u and at One Pusu. In the wider field of educational opportunity for boys and girls, however, there were far-reaching changes during those years. These new developments radically affected the people of the Solomons and the S.S.E.M.

In the pre-war Solomons, there had been no government schools for children. Not one. Little Maeliau did not go off to school the year he turned five. There was no primary school round the corner for him, no chalk talk, arithmetic, spelling, desks, discipline and schoolwork from 9 a.m. to 3 p.m. Schools like that simply did not exist—let alone free compulsory education for all the young. It is hard to imagine, like life without electric light.

No wonder the Marching Rule people made "good education" a major goal. After 57 years as a British Protectorate, in 1950 the Solomons had only one government school, established at Auki after the war, and the Islanders keenly felt their lack.

One Malu'u man, Arnon Atomea, felt a very specific interest. As a Marching Rule chief imprisoned at Gizo, he had caught the attention of Mr. Gregory-Smith, the Crown's representative who came there from England in May 1950.

"You Malaita people are wanting more education for your children," the visitor had said. "I think Arnon should start now to teach in school."

Arnon took him at his word. On his release from prison, the young Solomon Islander went immediately to the Auki school to learn the art of teaching. He became one of the first of his countrymen to be directly involved in government-sponsored education.

In among the children he sat, a young married man of 30, his quick mind absorbing the rudiments of arithmetic, English, social studies and science. With his keen glance and quiet smile, he was an apt, responsive pupil—watching the European teachers at work, and learning how they taught the children and managed discipline. Each afternoon he practiced teaching, and found he liked it.

With this and his earlier years at One Pusu as his entire training, Arnon started a school in 1952 for the children of his own Malu'u district. At first he had 30 or 40 boys and girls aged between 5 and 9, but the numbers soon rose to 70! His pupils would sit on the ground using their benches as writing desks. Arnon taught in their own language and in English, placing new words beside pictures or colors. The children would practice writing the words with chalk on black-painted masonite. They learned simple arithmetic, too, counting balls and sticks into bundles of ten.

Arnon taught five hours a day, between 8 a.m. and 2 p.m. In time, four other teachers joined him, and then he chose always to take the youngest class. He liked to lay the foundations himself in Standard 1. Gradually the pattern was changing: younger children, age-grading, several teachers, regular hours. Arnon's pupils were lucky. Very few children in the 1950s had even a taste of such education. For one out of two children, even today, there is still no schooling at all.

During the 1950s, the S.S.E.M. faced new ideas about its role in education. Originally, it had never set out to establish secular schools in the Solomons; the missionaries had come to help people like Peter Ambuofa spread the gospel among Islanders. But times and needs were changing. Christian leaders in the Solomons quietly made it clear that their people wanted the opportunity for schooling that would help them meet new developments as their country "grew up" towards independence. As the Christians greatly valued the spiritual element so strongly emphasized throughout past years, they wanted this education of their children to be provided within a Christian context. Therefore the leaders asked if the mission could develop a program to bring this about.

**148**

By 1960, the S.S.E.M. Directors had drawn up an Educational Program to meet the new demands. In outline, this program was a pyramid shape. At the base of the pyramid would be the village schools, 100 or more, providing junior primary education. From there, some pupils would go on to middle primary work at central boarding schools. These, in turn, would feed students into senior primary boarding schools, originally separate for boys and girls. Obviously, to start with, all students would be much older than "primary school age"; they would not even reach senior primary level until their late teens.

In the early 1960s, the teacher-missionaries really had to start from scratch. Schools had to be built, and those willing to try teaching needed a smattering of training. The missionary would introduce the basics: how to organize a school and set up a curriculum and schedule, how to start teaching simple arithmetic, English, singing, physical education, hygiene and natural science.

Diuna on Makira was a case in point. Here, a central boarding school would cater for children who came from the surrounding district, so all the villages were co-operating and some of the men were busy making desks and blackboard easels. It was back-breaking work, since they had no nails or prepared timber, and every piece had to be cut and adzed from the jungle. For desk-tops, they carved into the massive buttress-roots flaring out from the huge tree-trunks, and for desk-legs, they split bush poles and pegged them together in the absence of nails.

Other local men cut and carried vast loads of poles to build classrooms and houses for their new school. Then came the cutting of sage leaf to make the walls. The women, meanwhile, trekked doggedly back and forth to the beach, balancing on their heads the plaited-leaf baskets full of smooth pebbles. Day after day they toiled, carting the heavy loads of shingle to make roads and tracks for the school.

The Islanders threw themselves with a will into building

schools for their children, but they could not provide suitable teachers from among their own ranks. Too few had had any schooling. Young men with only four years of primary education as their total training found themselves struggling to teach children to that same level; yet there was no one else.

As Jim Dickson wrote in 1963, "In all our 100 village schools we haven't one fully trained school teacher." Jim was the mission's Education Director at the time, and his task was most necessary until Government District Education Officers were appointed in the mid-1960s. He continued: "We call them 'teachers', but really they are adult primary school pupils who have, at the best, reached standard six or seven level and are willing to begin the learning process among their people."

But he added: "It is grand to see the enthusiasm of our people for education and particularly now that they know that our aim is Christian education in the highest sense of the word. . . . Their desire is that God should be given His rightful place in all our educational planning and we know that to do less than this is to court disaster. Our Island leaders are awake to the pitfalls of education, but they are also aware of the needs and benefits of it."

Jotham Ausuta put it this way: "There is a very great need for a spiritual work among young people today. I have found that a boarding school, with spiritual Christian teachers, is a great thing. While we are giving our young ones education, we can plant in their minds and hearts the gospel of Christ who is the Way, the Truth and the Life."

Part of the plan was "localization": missionaries would work alongside Islanders and hand over full responsibility as soon as the Islanders had acquired sufficient training. Right from the beginning they would aim to work themselves out of one job—and into another. For example, a missionary would teach senior primary only until an Islander was available who was qualified to teach that

**150**

standard. By the late 1950s, the government had established a Teacher Training College at Honiara, and here, gradually, the teachers and principals of the future received their training; Arnon Atomea, for instance, studied there two years to gain his Grade 3 Certificate and become assistant head of the Auki government primary school.

During the 1960s the school at Su'u no longer gave Bible training to young men; it became a senior primary school for boys. At first, of course, the students were in their mid-teens because nearly everyone had a late start in schooling; and by 18 or 22, they were leaving school after six or seven years of primary education. Su'u was not then a high school.

Over the years, primary schools became established in many parts of the Solomons, and children could begin their education much younger. With complete primary schooling available elsewhere, by 1972 Su'u could become entirely a high school providing five years of secondary education to both boys and girls. Since very few Islanders were qualified to teach high school, most of the staff were teacher-missionaries.

Meanwhile, throughout the S.S.E.M. field, the mission's Education Secretary helped to foster the growth of primary schooling. By 1972, Ariel Famea was ready to take over this responsibility from Gwen Davies. His job included positioning teachers and paying them, allocating Government grants and arranging teachers' courses with the District Education Officcrs. The education program is designed to tie in closely with the government's plans and requirements, helping to co-ordinate schooling throughout the Islands.

John Maedola today would hardly recognize the schools and teachers of the Solomons. He himself was an unassuming man, "unlearned and ignorant" like Christ's first followers, but how he would rejoice to see the young children taught in Christian schools throughout his homeland!

*Regional Bible school principal preparing lesson*

# 17

# Bible
# Teaching for
# Changing
# Times

The Solomon Island pastor had a baffled look in his dark eyes. "We have always known the 'flesh' and the 'devil' here," he said slowly, "but this 'world' that is coming into the Solomons like a tide today—it is new to us, and we don't know how to meet it."

His comment summed up the feeling of many a pastor who was struggling to cope with new developments and rapid change. Soon, very soon, he and his fellow-Christians were to take over full charge of their Island church, and for that their training was inadequate. They had wide experience in dealing with village problems and people in trouble, but nothing to guide them in running a church that was to become self-governing. Their own faith in God was sturdy, but their young people had access to some disturbing new ideas, as influences from the outside world reached at last into the Solomons. Increasingly, during the 1950s, they felt the longing for further training and special refresher courses to keep up with the changing times.

To meet that new need, One Pusu became the center for short Leadership Courses for pastors during the early 1960s. Senior pastors came there to learn about governing a church, handling public moneys, and helping to keep nearly 300 local churches linked together. They put preaching and teaching into practice, and learned how to run effective Sunday Schools and Bible Classes. There was much to absorb in a brief time, and they eagerly drank in all they could.

Over the next ten years, One Pusu became a Training Institute for young men who wanted two years of specific Bible teaching. Then, in the early 1970s, a full-fledged Bible College came into being there. This new three-year program requires a higher standard of entrance to match the educational levels of today.

Meanwhile, to cater for the needs of many others who long to study God's Word, nine or more Regional Bible Schools have sprung up on three different islands. Like John Maedola's school in the 1930s, these are completely self-supporting and staffed entirely by Islanders.

To provide Bible training for girls of the Solomons, the Afio school was re-opened in 1948 after the war's disruption. From a tiny nucleus of five students, the school grew until 40 girls were boarding there once more for the two years of training. To begin with, new arrivals were mostly unschooled, and their teachers had to start with elementary reading skills.

During the years that followed, missionaries came and went at Afio, but Kadesh and Rachel Sikihi remained there as a continuing strength to the school. Kadesh, a quiet man of absolute integrity, gave devoted service in practical help and shouldered much responsibility. He took Sunday services and the early morning class, while his wife gave able assistance in teaching and in supervising the gardens. Until his death in 1962, Kadesh was like a father at Afio, a man who inspired trust.

**154**

One evening in 1959, the girls at Afio gathered in their school church for a very special occasion. Their bright eyes and smiles flashed in the light from the pressure lamp, as they crowded on to the benches, leaning forward eagerly.

Beth Filoa was talking to them, rather shy at all the attention. She remembered clearly her own days at Afio only a few years before. Now she was married, with a small daughter and another child on the way.

"I didn't mind leaving my people to go and be Jezreel's wife," she said, "because I think God chose me to marry him. Then, when we'd been married two weeks, Jezreel told me he was thinking of going to New Guinea for God. I said I was willing if God was calling us. We prayed, and God opened the way for us to go to One Pusu to prepare.

"Then I began to think how hard it is to leave my island, my home and my people. But God spoke one word to my heart in Matthew 19:29—'Everyone who has left houses and brothers or sisters or father or mother or children or lands, for my name's sake, will receive a hundredfold, and inherit eternal life.' This word comforted my heart, and I asked God to give me a great love for the women of New Guinea where we are going."

Jezreel and Beth went out as the very first missionaries sent by the budding Island church to a country overseas. They flew to the Sepik District near the north coast of New Guinea, where the S.S.E.M. had opened their second mission field in 1948. They went as Associate Missionaries, supported by their own people, and they gave 13 years of their lives to the people of New Guinea.

As education in the Solomons advanced, girls were able to attain senior primary levels and those who came to Afio had a better foundation on which their teachers could build. In 1964, Joan Gruber, who was in charge of Afio, felt the school could become a full Bible Institute for girls, and from that year, it kept parallel with the current One Pusu course, using the same lecture notes and teaching in English instead of Pidgin. To round out their education, the girls learn social studies and hygiene, mothercraft, homecraft, sewing and cooking. They love to sing, and practice often, and they also learn how to lead women's meetings, Bible studies and Sunday School.

The girls study Doctrine and most books of the Bible, using duplicated notes which become prized possessions. In their home villages, where books are rare, these study notes are very precious to the girls after training. Though the studies are put into simple words, this does not mean that they are in any sense "shallow." On the contrary, the girls often show a profound understanding of Scripture and a deep experience of God. They share in fellowship with each other, at meals or any time and most of them love and value their two years at Afio.

In 1974, complete responsibility for running the school was handed over to Islanders, and Unity Unasi was appointed Principal, with Mary Bili as her assistant. Both were former Afio students who had later graduated from the inter-mission Christian Leaders' Training College in Papua New Guinea.

Most ex-students of Afio are in villages or at home, but Beth Filoa was not the only one to go as a missionary across the sea to Papua New Guinea. Elizabeth, who had trained at Afio, went to the S.S.E.M. Sepik field when her husband, John Nake, became Principal of the Brugam Bible School there in 1974.

Mary Tehekau's home is the Polynesian island of Bellona, small neighbor to Rennell and far to the south of the Solomons group in the wide loneliness of the Pacific. Her people, tall and golden-skinned, live always within earshot of the pounding breakers, for their island measures only six miles by two. Mary left her home and her close-knit family for years of training and experience, first at Afio and then in Papua New Guinea. From the Christian Leaders' Training College, she went on to join the staff at the Yagrumbok

**156**

Girls' Bible School in the Sepik field.

So the good seed of the Word sown in the Solomon Islands continues to bear fruit through the lives of Islanders not only at home but in Papua New Guinea.

*Island baptism*

# 18

# The
# Young Church
# Comes
# of Age

"How does this next statement sound, do you think?" Ken Griffiths cleared his throat and read from the draft copy prepared by the S.S.E.M. Sydney Council for consideration: " 'The aim of the mission is to bring into being churches which from the outset are self-governing, self-supporting and self-propagating.' "

It was 1957, and in the small office near the heart of noisy Sydney, Australia, the other S.S.E.M. Directors considered the statement thoughtfully. The matter under revision was *Principles and Practice of the S.S.E.M.*, the written guidelines and rules of the mission. In this statement, the Directors wanted to make clear the principles of "localization" that had guided the mission for many years.

The small Board of Directors had been in charge of the mission for only a comparatively short time. From 1904 until her death in 1940, it was Florence Young who had visited and superintended the mission from her home base in Sydney, assisted by the S.S.E.M. Council there. During the war years, changes were obviously necessary, and late in 1943 the S.S.E.M. acquired legal recognition as an incorporated body under the guidance of a Board of Directors. Policy and administration were in the Directors' hands, and all their decisions had to be completely unanimous.

"Yes," one of them commented. "I think that statement's good. We want to get across the ultimate goal. The mission is there at the moment to teach and help Islanders in whatever ways it can, specially in Bible training, but we want to encourage the people there to take on full responsibility for running their own church and sharing the gospel with their own countrymen."

Across the table, another Director had something to add: "I think you could sum it up like this—what we want to see is the indigenous church growing up in the Solomons, and coming of age. We want to see it reach a stage where it can stand on its own feet. That's the aim, and I think it's summed up concisely and accurately in that statement."

The church in the Solomon Islands needed time and nurture for its gradual growth towards maturity. Just as an individual grows from babyhood and utter dependence through childhood and adolescence to responsible adulthood, so it was with the Island church. At every stage of that development, there were Solomon Islanders who were mature Christians, deeply taught of God: men like Clement Maelalo and John Maedola. But the church as a functioning body needed many years of growth and teaching until it came of age.

From the very beginning, it had always been the Islanders themselves who had gone out to establish local churches among their own people. These evangelists and teacher-pastors supported themselves, building their bush-timber houses and growing their own food-crops like everyone else. The mission gave them support by encouraging them, helping and teaching them, and by praying with them and for them in the problems that arose.

Right from the start, then, Solomon Islanders shouldered the task of taking the gospel to those who had not heard, often staying for years to teach and shepherd new Christians. In those days, however, they did not have the responsibility of receiving new Christians into the fellowship of the visible church; it was always a missionary who examined people for baptism and then took the service.

When Ahikaupaine, for instance, chose to break with his past way of life and came to live in the Christian village at Taka Taka, it was the teacher-pastor, Edwin, who gave him daily teaching in the little church there. At least two years of this regular instruction were considered necesssary before the newcomer could be regarded as ready for baptism. Edwin, meanwhile, had every chance to see the change in Ahikaupaine's way of life, and he would know very well if the former cannibal had become a "new creation", putting his trust in Christ instead of the *akalo* worship.

By 1934, Edwin felt that Ahikaupaine was ready for the step of baptism. When the visiting missionary came on the *Evangel* in September, Edwin was present while each of the eleven new Christians was asked searching questions to make sure that each one was ready for baptism. Then, after a brief service in the little church, everyone gathered on the shingle beach for the baptismal service, and Edwin prayed in the local language.

Two lines of candidates stood ready to step forward: six men and five women; and Ahikaupaine was the third to wade into the water towards the waiting missionary.

"Joash, I baptize you in the name of the Father, and of the Son, and of the Holy Spirit." The words were spoken in deep reverence.

After his baptism in the sea, Joash Ahikaupaine came up out of the water to join the Christians gathered on the shore. In the church once more, afterwards, the newly baptized men and women received the Lord's Supper for the first time, and were welcomed into the full fellowship of the Church.

The Lord's Supper, as it was always called, was also held regularly on the first Sunday in every month, and then of course it was the pastor-teacher Edwin who would take the service. For "bread" he used the staple food of the Solomons: taro, or yam. The "wine" was the juice of the pierced green coconut, poured into individual "cups" made of folded leaf.

A pastor like Edwin greatly valued visits from the nearest missionary and from those on board the *Evangel*. Apart from that, his only link with other churches was the monthly day of fellowship when he met with other pastors in his district to talk over problems, and to pray. Before the 1950s, there was no general church organization, no pattern of having local church officers to help shoulder responsibility.

In the changing atmosphere of the early 1950s, the Directors of the S.S.E.M. took steps to encourage the formation of a simple framework—needed by then as a means of linking together nearly 300 village churches. For the first time, each local church was to have officers to share the pastoral and business responsibilities of that particular church. These would meet once a month. In addition, groups of local churches (perhaps 20 which shared a common language) were to be linked together in Associations of churches, whose representatives would meet twice a year. These District Associations were to consider the work of God in their whole district, and they were each to have a President, Vice-President and Secretary—roles entirely new to the Solomon Islanders. Through Marching Rule, the Island people had shown their capacity for organization, but properly constituted meetings were a mystery to them. They knew nothing about the keeping of written records and accounts. For even the simplest form of church organization, they needed some guidance, training and experience.

"This matter of how to handle money," one of them said, "It's like a great dark cloud over us. We simply must know more about that, and we must understand everything else that's involved in running the church in this new way." So

**162**

to help organize the church in this new pattern, the mission Directors invited an experienced former missionary, Rev. William Gibbins, to visit each district with Timothy Anilafa.

"Don't forget," Mr. Gibbins would advise the Islanders, "when you are President of a District Association, don't let everybody talk 'all about.' It's your job to control the meeting. Keep a good spirit in it, and a time-limit. You remember the old kind of meeting where people went on talking till daylight—with nothing decided. That's no use! No good every bit."

The Islanders appreciated Mr. Gibbins' help and advice, and they were willing and ready for this new step towards full responsibility. Timothy Anilafa, who traveled with Mr. Gibbins, helped to communicate all the new concepts to his own people.

Timothy proved to be just the man to take on the exacting new job of General President of all the Associations. For years he had been assisting at the One Pusu training center, and so was well and widely known. People trusted and respected him. He had long ago given up this world's ambitions and opportunities to follow God's will for his life, and like his close friend, John Maedola, he did not swing in with the Marching Rule movement; yet afterwards, retaining the confidence and respect of his fellow-Islanders, he was enabled by God to become a vital link between the mission and the adolescent church. His wise and understanding wife, Elizabeth, was a tremendous strength to him.

For the ten years following 1953, the Islanders had the opportunity to gain practical experience in church organizations. They assumed full responsibility for examining baptismal candidates and for baptizing them, and they continued to learn how to work together in their Associations. So that the missionaries, too, could keep closely in touch with the new development, an Advisory Committee of senior missionaries and Island leaders was formed in 1958.

To develop any new working relationship between people

takes time. When Rev. Festo Kivengere from Africa visited the Solomons in 1959, he recognized a continuing tendency towards separation into two camps. A greater depth of fellowship was needed, and closer co-operation between missionaries and Island leaders. So in 1960, there was a special conference of missionaries and church leaders to give the opportunity for intermingling and fellowship among all present. There was a dawning recognition of the need to share together, eat together, and talk on a brother-to-brother basis, with no dividing into two separate groups and no paternalism.

"At the end of our three days' Conference," wrote Jotham Ausuta, "joy, peace and unity filled our hearts. We found out in ourselves that fellowship or oneness is not an easy thing. It costs humility and openness. We believe that only when we Christians are willing to be humble and open with others in our hearts, can there be real fellowship. A real fellowship brings revival to the church. This is our deep desire for the Island Church."

Jotham's words about what must happen before revival were truer than he knew.

As the scattered tribes of the Solomons continued to grow towards nationhood, the many local churches of the S.S.E.M. saw increasingly their need to be strongly linked together. They prayed that someone spiritually mature and experienced in church affairs would come to help guide their growing young Church, and give leadership training.

In Sydney, early in 1963, Rev. Bert Hawley read of this special need, and thought it over one day while mowing his lawn. He had served many years as a missionary in Peru and as a minister in Australia, and—though he was 60—he became convinced that God wanted him in the Solomons. By the middle of the year, he and his wife were on the S.S.E.M. staff in the Islands, and for six months he visited each district with the mission Field Secretary. They discussed with the people the full significance of a very special conference

**164**

arranged for March 1964.

This Conference was to be both a final step and a new beginning. For the very first time, representatives from the whole S.S.E.M. area gathered together at Ambu on Malaita for a week's conference. From Rennell, Bellona, Makira, Guadalcanal, the Russell Islands plantations, and all over Malaita came the 53 delegates—on foot, by canoe, or by ship. A group of missionaries and two Directors arrived from One Pusu on the *Evangel*, which anchored within a stone's throw of Ambu village. The gleaming ripples of the harbor reflected coconut palms, leaf-roofed houses, and excited children.

Right on the water's edge, near the canoe-house, was a mighty sign with "WELCOME" outlined in vivid red hibiscus blooms. As the visitors stepped ashore, their hands were gripped by eager handshakes. They climbed the path to the huge church that was already thronged with people: the local villagers, and the delegates from the 20 District Associations who represented 282 villages. Here, in the week that followed, Islanders and missionaries discussed in detail every aspect of a church constitution. There was a spirit of exceptional harmony, unspoiled by any discord, and in this atmosphere all the creative ideas that emerged could be discussed. When a workable constitution had been hammered out, it was adopted unanimously.

When they came to choosing a name for their church, three suggestions given by Islanders were written on the blackboard for all to consider. The name *South Sea Evangelical Church* was chosen for two reasons: the Islanders wanted to keep as close as possible to the name that had joined them for 60 years, and they wanted a name that would equally suit the young church in the Papua New Guinea field, if it wished to share the same name.

The missionaries thought that the newly named church should have a Solomon Islander as its first president, but the delegates had other ideas. They were convinced that

**165**

they needed someone with more experience to guide them through their first year, so unanimously they elected Rev. Bert Hawley to that position. To act on behalf of the General Conference till it met again in a year's time, they elected the other officers and members of the Executive. The Conference closed with an opening service on Sunday, March 8th, the official inauguration of the South Sea Evangelical Church. More than 1300 packed the building to overflowing, and Jemuel Afia spoke on the text "Christ loved the Church and gave Himself for it."

Exactly 60 years after Florence Young first sighted the island of Malaita, the young church established there had finally come of age. In the years between, some 15,000 believers in Christ had been baptized, and the church was on its way towards spiritual maturity.

*George Strachan*

# 19

# Renewed
# in
# The
# Spirit

"Coming of age" in 1964 brought no instant cure to the church's problem. The newly-elected leaders had a deep concern for those in their care, and a growing sense of need. Times were changing in the Solomons, in ways not for the better.

In the past, Island Christians had known first-hand God's supernatural power. Taking Him at His Word, some, by faith, had even cast out demons and healed the sick in Jesus' Name. To their children and grandchildren, however, such experiences were very second-hand.

For the younger generation, in particular, life in the Solomons was becoming more complex and sophisticated. The possession of "things" loomed larger, and some, drawn by the magnet of materialism, craved education as the key to jobs and leadership. Few were ready and wiling to take on responsibility in the S.S.E.C.

Some of the church leaders remembered the touch of the Holy Spirit in the late 1930s, when He came in cleansing and renewing power. They felt that nothing less than His touch again would satisfy their own hearts and bring full life to the church.

Time and again, they had arranged for conventions and crusades with good speakers. People would respond and repent, and the results would seem encouraging. But they did not last.

Increasingly, both missionaries and Islanders prayed from their hearts for God's reviving power in the church. At Afio, for example, ten or fifteen or more girls would be on their feet praying at the one time, as the spirit of prayer came upon their gathering. (This "united prayer" did not seem unusual or confusing to the Islanders, since God hears each individual.) For more than a year, the praying continued to build up.

In April, 1970, a letter went out to all S.S.E.C. pastors, representing nearly 300 local churches: "Muri Thompson, a Maori evangelist from New Zealand, will be here for a number of crusades during July and August. . . . Have your people pray every day. . . . Now is the time to start praying. What should we pray for? Revival, a mighty pouring out of God's Holy Spirit upon His people so that people from all churches and missions will be eternally built up in Christ . . . So that every one who carries the name of Christian will make Jesus his Lord and Master forever. Only as God's Spirit comes upon us will this everlasting work be done. God is sick of this "getting right" for a little time and then drifting back into sin. Let us pray that in these crusades lives will be changed forever. Today start praying."

The people responded. Many had already been praying. Now, specifically, they prayed for the coming crusades, for Muri Thompson, and for his team.

Beginning with Honiara, Muri spent two months visiting centers on all the islands with a team of Christian leaders. During the first month, they held meetings in the Russell Islands, on the south coast of Guadalcanal, in the islands of Rennell and Bellona, at Kira Kira on Makira, and at Ro'one and Riverside on South Malaita. Those weeks together travelling on the *Evangel* proved to be a time of preparation. On board were all the main S.S.E.C. leaders, Muri Thompson and his team of two Maoris, and one missionary, George Strachan. They had the opportunity of getting to know and understand each other as fellowmembers of a team, and this was most important.

After one month, half-way through the series of crusades, Muri was speaker at the annual Mission's Field Conference, held at One Pusu during the first week of August. The night before the first meeting there, Muri mentioned to George that no one had ever told him he was to preach to missionaries. "I don't know what to give you," he said.

From the very first meeting on the Monday morning, however, it was obvious that God was in control because of the liberty with which Muri ministered, and the power that came through God's Word. All the missionaries were present, together with Island leaders of the S.S.E.C.

At that conference, the Holy Spirit began to work in a new way, and He went deep. Muri's messages were not emotional, but one man present broke down and cried and cried, utterly broken before God, confessing sins of bitterness, animosity and resentment. Another quietly went back 23 years, confessing a sin of attitude then that had never been put right with God and with missionaries.

In a quiet and orderly way, God convicted missionaries and Island leaders of wrong attitudes, resentful thoughts, hurt feelings, jealousies and other sins of the spirit which had been hindering unity and crippling God's work, in some cases for years. They confessed openly, and asked forgiveness of God and of each other in true brokenness.

As Gordon Wilson wrote at the time, "There is no more shattering experience than to be humbled to the dust in public, in an agony of sin and failure, but what joy and praise follows the release of the burden.... It was a deeply moving experience, and the love shed abroad in our hearts was tremendous."

It was unmistakably a work of the Holy Spirit, and all present were affected. God Himself was bringing the leaders of the mission and the church into a right relationship with each other and with Him. He was preparing the way for a deep and wide movement throughout the Islands.

Following the conference, Muri Thompson continued with the crusades, as arranged, travelling with a team of about 40 that included the Maori, John Pipi, Solomon Islanders and missionaries. As they visited centers around Malaita during the next two weeks, the power of the Holy Spirit became increasingly evident. At Kwaiana, for example, when the forces of opposition showed out in demon possession, God's power prevailed, and the evil spirits were cast out.

George Strachan, who was in the team travelling on board the *Evangel*, said, "We found it essential that there be nothing, absolutely nothing, coming between any of us. Within the team, God brought everything out so that we were able to be in deep fellowship with each other and with the Lord. I have never known such fellowship.

"This is extremely important: God works through His body, and if the body is not functioning together, then the Spirit of God is hindered. If ever the Spirit didn't move in a meeting, then afterwards we in the team would bring out everything that we could think of—seemingly little things, often—and following that, the Spirit would come quickly, moving in our midst in the meetings, as if He couldn't wait to bless us.

"The 'little' things that might hinder the Spirit might include sins of attitude, such as grievances or criticisms. One of us might have thought that somebody else had spoken against him, and often it might turn out to be a mis-understanding. Or someone might confess, 'Yesterday I said something against my brother here'."

By the time the team reached Kobiloko on the north-east

**172**

coast of Malaita, there was a growing sense of spiritual anticipation. On the second day, God's power showed in unusual conviction of sin and an increasing spirit of praise, but no one expected what was about to happen.

Sunday morning came, August 23, and Kath Crouch was among those gathered in the church ready for the service. "John Pipi, (who, when he sings, makes you think of Stephen —his face just shines) began singing," she wrote. "The Spirit seemed to come upon many, breaking hearts down before the Lord."

Many were crying, and leaders were disturbed that they could not stop it. Ariel Bili and Arnon Sau went to meet those coming ashore from the *Evangel* which was anchored close to the beach, inside the reef. Muri Thompson, George Strachan and Jemuel Afia were on their way to join the others for the meeting. As they stepped from the dinghy on to the wide black sand beach, Arnon and Ariel told them of what was already happening in the church.

They walked together up to the church, along the pebbly track edged with shrubs. As Ariel and Arnon shared their concern about the people in distress, it became clear that this was the "godly sorrow" of deep repentance. The leaders were relieved, and those crying were taken to a separate building while the meeting commenced.

Those weeping were in great distress. In the back seat, one girl was crying, "Oh, my sin, my sin!" and George Strachan told her, "Jesus died for your sins. Accept forgiveness by faith." The Holy Spirit evidently took the word and applied it, for she stopped crying immediately and said "Praise God!" with her hands raised high. The leaders dealt with each in need, until the weeping had turned to great joy, and they soon rejoined the meeting.

The church was leaf-thatched and earth-floored, with the roof extended so that about 600 people could crowd on to the benches and hear the speaker. That morning, Muri preached a powerful message, and then said, "If anyone wants to come forward. . . ." At this, the whole congregation got up and surged forward, and many broke into strong crying, both men and women. One senior pastor was there, right in the front, with tears streaming down his cheeks like a little boy.

They were left for perhaps ten minutes, and then Muri said, just once, "Praise the Lord". There was total response, and outbursts of joy and praise spread over the whole gathering and continued for another fifteen minutes.

"It was tremendous, such as I have never seen or heard in all my life," wrote George Strachan. "The whole situation was in the perfect control of the Holy Spirit: no hysteria, no panic—simply joy unspeakable and full of glory. The Holy Spirit came down. God was visiting His people."

Many saw visions when God met them. Many saw Jesus on the Cross; others saw Him on the Throne. Some saw angels, or a very bright light. Some spoke in tongues, and a few received healing, but most told of how they had seen the Lord afresh and come into a new experience of Him. All seemed to appreciate the need for a constant humility and a sensitivity to the Holy Spirit.

Those in the team were full of joy, but they wondered what would happen at Sifolo, the next center. The Koio people there were by nature wild and excitable, and the Island leaders prayed earnestly that God would keep full control.

On the steep west side of the large Uru harbor is the village of Sifolo, home for 150 people. Their church is large, but in great expectation they had extended it sideways and lengthwise to hold about 2000 people. Many people had arrived on foot and by canoe to attend the meetings. As the *Evangel* anchored, canoes clustered round and the people looked up with wondering faces. Everyone on the ship seemed to be singing.

The visitors came by dinghy through the mangrove stumps and muddy water, to step ashore at the root-stump landing. The flat grassy area near the church was crowded with people eager to greet them. More than 2000 had assembled and once again, there were two full days during which the Holy Spirit prepared the hearts of those present; there was a growing conviction of sin among the people, and a widespread longing to be filled with the Spirit. The team of leaders were deeply concerned about maintaining perfect oneness in the Spirit, and the slightest cause of disunity was openly dealt with. No cloud must be allowed to remain between any of them, and two points of conflicting opinion were faced up to with humility and straightforwardness.

On August 27, the team went into the meeting clear of disunity, so far as they knew, and with a deep sense of harmony among them. After giving his message, Muri Thompson asked for a time of silent prayer. In the hush that followed, he heard a sound.

"At first," he said, "I thought it was audible prayer among the congregation, but realized it was above, in the distance, like a wind, and getting louder.

"I looked up through an opening in the leaf roof to the heavens from where the sound seemed to be coming. It grew to a roar—then it came to me: surely this is the Holy Spirit coming like a mighty rushing wind. I called the people to realize that God the Holy Spirit was about to descend upon them."

Outside, three of the leaders were up the sharply rising hillside in a small prayer house, very nearby but higher. They noticed the silence as they listened, and came outside. Then they heard the noise: it was not everywhere—it was just immediately above the church.

George Strachan, inside the church, at first dismissed the sound as being an airplane far away. But as it came closer, he thought, "What's that? Is it a gale glowing up?" Thinking of the ship at anchor with only one man aboard, he looked out to see if the trees were moving—but their leaves were perfectly still. Then he thought, "This is the Holy Spirit coming as at Pentecost!"

In a matter of seconds, the silent church started to echo

with wailing, praying and strong crying. As the leaders gave praise aloud, cries of conviction increased among the people. Gradually, they started to come through to deliverance. There was no panic; hardly anyone moved from his seat. All was under the control of God.

Within a week, the crusades came to an end, and Muri Thompson returned from Honiara to New Zealand. There were no further gatherings organized, but the work of the Spirit in the Solomons had only just begun.

# 20

# The Fire Spreads

After Muri Thompson left the Solomons, teams of Christian men started visiting around Malaita and other islands. As they went, the outpouring and power of the Holy Spirit went with them.

At the One Pusu Bible Institute, there had been a steady, continuing movement of the Spirit ever since the August conference. In September, Ed Nash, the Principal wrote: "For the last four weeks we have not had a regular school. Lectures have been interrupted simply by the Spirit taking over. This has been evident by the conviction and prayer that has been upon us."

On one occasion, a student sprang to his feet and said very determinedly, "I want to give my life to Christ every bit." That evening, he went to see Ed, and spoke next day of what he had done. It was so sincere and Spirit-led that it released the Spirit. Others spoke until, without warning, sobs broke out.

One boy stood and said, "Excuse me," but he got no further. The conviction was such that only after several minutes did he sob out, "Lord have mercy on me." Then another started.

It was not confusion—rather it was a deep experience of the Holy Spirit coming into the classroom. The boys were sobbing uncontrollably, but Ed asked others present to deal with them. Even though they were fellow-students, these men were so in touch with God that they could handle the situation, and lead the others into a place of assurance and peace.

"It was all so orderly, and so full of joy and praise," wrote Ed, "that one is not left in doubt as to who was doing it all. It had no leader but the Spirit. We can only praise God for what has happened and is happening. Join us."

From Afio Bible Institute for Girls, Joan Gruber wrote: "We asked God that all here would be 'filled with the Spirit'. He answered abundantly and 'delivered us from all our fears'. I was amazed as I heard students testify of being delivered from all kinds of fears: fear of other people, fear of sickness and death, fear of speaking out, fear of the future, and even fear of me! Now, instead, we 'exalt His Name together.' What a difference it makes when one is released and controlled by the Holy Spirit. The fruit of the Spirit, such as love, joy and peace, is so evident in all lives.

" 'The humble hear and are glad'. It is evident in revival that the Lord only meets those who know their need and are willing to be truly humble—to confess even the smallest sin and make restitution where necessary.

"There seems to be real conviction of sin, and willingness to put it right. Today, one woman walked for four hours, crossing two big rivers, to pay for a cake of soap she had taken long ago. And a man asked me for a missionary's address, as he was cross with her in 1952.

"The teams that have visited this school have been so wise and humble and led of the Spirit. One man here is outstanding: sensitive to the Spirit, gracious and loving. The Lord

**178**

used him with the others, too, as a real team.

"After these men have proclaimed the Word, there is usually a long time of counseling many, so that all are cleansed and ready for the fulness of the Spirit. Then, at another meeting, the team explain about the Spirit, and what He wants to do in each one.

"When they ask all to pray that the Lord will fill them, and the people pray, it is then that many young folk see visions of the Lord dying for them, or glorified, or visions of heaven or angels (this is often a child's vision). Some see gross darkness, and then bright lights; some see nothing at all.

"Then all are praising God, singing choruses of praise, and flooded with joy. In this part of the world, they all sing with movement—waving their hands and beating time. It just seems suitable. They are so full of joy and love for the Lord and for others that they cannot contain themselves, and tell of Him to all they meet.

"There has been tremendous joy in sharing with others, who have seen what God has done for these students, and have wanted the same joy. It is almost overwhelming to watch the way the Holy Spirit works through any who are humble and give Him all the glory."

Afio is on the island of South Malaita, a place where the Enemy had long held some Christian villages in bondage. At Ro'one and Supaine, for instance, the people grew special trees to use the fragments of leaf, bark or wood as fetishes or charms. Every child had to have its own parcel of these, for protection from the evil powers of others, for everybody feared everyone else. One man had gathered 50 or more such fetishes which he would use to get power over money, fishing, rain, wind, stealing, killing, seducing—and for his own protection.

In mid-October, 1970, a team of seven Islanders visited South Malaita, spending time in each village. They preached the Word clearly, and the Holy Spirit worked in conviction, breaking down hearts that had been cold and clogged with sin and compromise for years. During their visit, the Spirit reached parts of the Church in South Malaita that had never been touched and cleansed before. At one village, when the Holy Spirit came in conviction and power, the people afterwards filled two and a half baskets with their fetishes for the team to pray over and throw into the sea. Because of these fetishes, evil powers had been active in these people's lives for many years, and all through South Malaita there was much casting out of demons.

In the village of Heraniesi, the people brought along Wawai, the young man from another village who had never been able to hear or speak. He could only call. The team needed great faith in praying for him, but in the end he began to hear, and to speak words like a small child. He was not the only one to receive healing. As Jonathan Manepuri wrote six years later: "Many of the people in our churches were healed, too. From 1970 until today they have remained better."

One member of the team that went to South Malaita was a pastor called Jeriel Tahioa, and his own story is illuminating.

"Though we had been praying hard for revival," he said, "when revival came we were very surprised. At the Conference in August, Muri had preached on Acts. He compared our coming together there at One Pusu with those who gathered in Jerusalem, when the Spirit of God came upon them, and then they went out into other places later on.

"So it was with us. But at first when the power of God came upon the people in my church, I didn't feel anything. Nothing happened, nothing filled me; I felt empty. When my fellow church leaders prayed over me for me to have power to help in the work, no power came. I prayed hard about this, and I was worried.

"One thing I knew, when they prayed I was afraid and

**180**

thought, 'What kind of power is this? I haven't heard of it or seen it before.' I had been in the heathen before, and had feared the devil's powers. And now I was afraid of God. I thought, 'If I'm not good enough in my work, with this new power, if I go wrong—I might die.'

Because of this fear, I did not get the blessing others were receiving. I was troubled, and cried 'Why not me? Everyone else is happy.'

One night I woke about 4:30 a.m., feeling troubled, and prayed. Then I woke up another church leader who was staying with us. He said it was the time to pray. 'You trust the Master?' he asked. 'You ask the Master yourself.' So I prayed, and he prayed over me, and something came—I was sobbing, and my heart was like a fire, and then I was full of joy and singing. This was the first time the Lord had met me like that.

"But two days later, when I grieved the Holy Spirit, I found the power gone. I was weak like an empty rice bag that can't stand up. I thought of King Saul—and I didn't want the Spirit of the Lord to go and an evil spirit to come. I couldn't eat or sleep. But when my friend came back and prayed for me, and I confessed what the Holy Spirit had convicted me about, then the power and joy came back.

"Another time, when I prayed for something not right, I was immediately conscious that the gift had gone, so I called for another to pray for me, and confessed, and the Spirit of God was with me. Every time my thinking or talking was not true, or I was hard to my children, I became conscious that I had grieved the Holy Spirit.

"This continued, and I knew that I must give my body, heart, soul and mind every bit—as it says in Ephesians 5:18 'Be filled with the Spirit,' not just filled once. During August, September, October, I was still not strong. I would confess, as in 1 John 1:9 'If we confess our sins, He is faithful and just to forgive us our sins and to cleanse us from all unrighteousness.' Then the power would come back. But I struggled much with my Master. It was not until He had tested me many times that I was ready to go with the team to South Malaita.

About that time, another Solomon Island Christian wrote: "It is a joy to tell you that the outpouring and power of the Holy Ghost is everywhere in the Solomons among those who are hungry for the power and blessing of God these days. It is more than words can express.

"When the Spirit came upon them with power, love and joy, people could pray and sing glory to Jesus from midnight to daylight, and never notice it as a long time.

"Many of them have seen visions, when the Spirit has come upon them. Different people see different visions. Some were humbled by their visions, and cried with deep sorrow for their sin, when seeing Christ hanging on the cross, with His pierced hands, head, feet and side. At the same time, they saw how sinful they were, and cried and cried, sometimes very loud, with closed eyes facing upward to the cross of Christ."

One Islander, a senior policeman in Honiara, became a changed man, and experienced a vision that was remarkable. One Saturday night, he saw a vision of weeping children, and was told, "These are the children of the man you put in prison last week."

This was a man accused of stealing a radio from his employer's house. Though he claimed that another man was guilty, he could not name or describe the other man. Since a cover of the radio was found in the house of the accused, the senior policeman in judging the case found him guilty and gave him six months in prison.

In his vision, the senior policeman was shown the guilty man, his house and name. Early next morning, he was not at church; he was visiting the given house, and asking for the man by name.

"That's me," said the man at the door.

"You are the man who stole the radio," said the policeman, and the man at the door confessed that he was guilty. The innocent man was soon released from prison.

Japhlet, another Honiara man, was closely involved in follow-up team work after the crusades were over. He said, "While I am writing this letter, a verse in the prophet Joel 2:28 comes to my mind: 'In the last days, I will pour out my Spirit upon all flesh.' I believe that this has been fulfilled in the Solomons at this time.

"After the Crusades, follow-up teams have been going around the Islands. Our Honiara follow-up team visited several villages on Guadalcanal. As I went along with them, I saw real breaking through, deep conviction of sin, and joy full of glory as the blessing of God poured out into many villages. Many lives have met Christ for the very first time, and some for restoration. Demons have been cast out in the Name of Jesus.

"I remember a young man who was possessed with five demons. The first time we prayed over him, nothing happened. We prayed again for the second time, when I remembered what Peter and John did for the impotent man at the Beautiful Gate. They used the Name of Jesus.

"So I prayed, 'In the Name of Jesus Christ, I command this demon to leave this man.'

"After I said that prayer, the demons left the young man, and he burst out crying and the Holy Spirit convicted him of all his sins. From that moment, he opened his heart and invited the Lord Jesus Christ to come into his heart. I can remember that young man prayed and asked God to forgive him of all his wrongdoings. The Holy Spirit filled this man's heart, and now he is singing and praising God every day. Glory and honor to Jesus Christ alone."

Japhlet's final comment finds an echo in a letter from Muri Thompson after his return to New Zealand: " . . . .we want to give all of the Glory to the Lord our God. This has been His doing and it is marvelous in our eyes. He has said He will not share His Glory with another, and we can only thank Him from the depth of our being for the rich and unique privilege which has been ours to observe His power in operation. . . . We can only say that we had not the faintest idea of what would transpire during our tour of the Solomons. What was our privilege to witness has never been our experience ever before, and we can only give Glory to God that He has seen fit to pour out His Spirit in a magnitude never before realized in our experience. . . . We say quite categorically that this has been entirely the Lord's doing, we have only been instruments in His Hands as He has seen fit to use. And any suggestion that some of this has been the result of human effort is only to detract from the total Glory of the Lord our God. To Him alone be all the Praise."

In that same letter, Muri made this comment: "There are always those who will be uncertain as to a movement of this nature, particularly in relation to the spectacular and to the supernatural dimension. . . ."

David Irofanua at Fo'ondo was one of those; he had definite doubts and reservations. He had never seen anything like it before, so as pastor he would not allow his church to join in. Some went elsewhere—and gradually David saw the hardened lives of some of his people being changed. His own son was transformed, and one night David saw in a dream a branch bearing fruit in the far distance, while near at hand was a dry stump. He realized that he had despised the work of the Holy Spirit, and that God was doing a *new* thing in the last days, and that all should join in with it.

In June 1971, he said publicly, "Yes, I'm willing now. I understand that His way is not our way. Before, I prayed that if this movement were not of the Lord, it would stop. But it did not stop; it went on—but it jumped over my church."

He spoke of his dream, and he confessed his hardness. The Spirit of the Lord came in power upon his church, with the sound of a rushing mighty wind, as at Sifolo. David was a

**184**

strong man, never able to cry. But he cried after confessing his hardness. He said afterwards, "I was crying only because I was rejoicing in God's mercy. If God were a man, He would have just left me far behind. But He is not a man, so He has come back and given revival here in my church—the joy that I missed a year ago."

*Island prayer meeting*

# 21

# The Spirit Who Is Holy

It was 4 a.m., and the tiny islet of Nongosila was still shrouded in darkness. Two visitors sleeping in one of the leaf-walled houses woke up to the gong-like sound of the church "bell," a metal cylinder. They dressed quickly, and joined the people outside walking softly along the sandy path to the church.

The sand-floored church was already half full, and men and women were slipping in quietly, taking their places on the long benches. A single pressure-lamp threw light on the face of a young man at the reading-stand. He was leading the singing with simple reverence, but his voice was still not quite awake and a little creaky.

When all had gathered, somebody prayed in the local language, and the young man spoke about a Bible verse or two. It was his job that day to lead the time of prayer.

Then every person in the church began to pray aloud and fervently, each praying his own prayer to God who could hear each one. To the listening visitors, it sounded like the ebb and flow of a surging sea, the sound of many waters, surging to a climax and subsiding. Each prayed for cleansing, and then for the wider needs of the church. Some spoke in their own dialect, some used Pidgin and some English. They were oblivious of each other, thinking only of the Lord.

The young man at the front brought that time of prayer to a close, and announced a brief hymn. Then again everyone prayed out loud, some speaking in tongues this time, before the meeting was brought to a conclusion.

In many villages on Malaita, a time like this for early morning prayer each day has become part of life's new pattern since the revival. One village woman had been accustomed to going each morning until she had a new baby, and was unable to go. She said, "When I hear the church bell sound, I *want* to go. I miss it."

There is a new longing to pray, a new hunger for God's Word, and a new sensitivity to the Spirit who is Holy.

Jotham Ausuta once said, "The Holy Spirit is unable to fill the life that has some sin harbored in it. The Holy Spirit is so very sensitive—about things we might consider unimportant.

"Travelling in Papua New Guinea recently, I was sharing a room with Jesimiel, and I found myself unable to sleep. There was something in my heart, but I thought, 'It's nothing that matters. Why should I tell Jesimiel, anyway? He doesn't know anything about it.'

"But I tossed and turned, until Jesimiel asked what was the matter. 'Oh, I just can't sleep,' I said, trying to cover it up. But then I told him, and said, 'Will you forgive me?' 'But it's as nothing to me!' said Jesimiel. But we prayed together, and then peace came back to me, and I slept soundly.

"The Holy Spirit, we find, is very, very sensitive. In the Solomons, we say that His blessing in our lives is like an egg that we must hold carefully. If we let it drop, it's gone. Or we say that it is like bringing back stream-water to our friends working in the food-garden. We carry the water in a taro

**188**

leaf, so we must take care not to let anything pierce the leaf, or the water will run out. Even a little hole will prevent our friends' thirst being quenched."

George Strachan put it this way: "To me, revival is truth becoming alive and powerful. Ordinarily, we might say 'God is good' and we mean it. But for the goodness and holiness of God to really come home to us, we need the ministry of the Spirit. Then the truth hits us with such impact that the very goodness of God overwhelms us utterly. It is the same when it comes to conviction of sin. When these truths become a reality, the contrast between our own sin and God's righteousness is completely overwhelming.

"Our experience at One Pusu was only a beginning. When the conviction of sin came there, it was a humbling experience for everyone, having to confess one to another. We felt it very much.

"But at Kobiloko, it was something entirely different. Like Isaiah, the people saw the holiness of God, and their reaction was 'Woe is me! For I am lost; for I am a man of unclean lips, and I dwell in the midst of a people of unclean lips . . .' Having seen the Lord, they saw themselves; and they wept, saying 'My sin, my sin!' That experience went far deeper than our experience at One Pusu. It was different, and it led to deliverance in a different way: a realization of God and a release from themselves."

Speaking from his own first-hand experience of this, Michael Maeliau said on one occasion:

"People have often asked me, 'How did you feel in the revival?' and my answer has always been one word, 'Transparent'.

"I felt that somebody was looking right through me, and that there was nothing in me that could be hidden any more.

"Why was this? It was a time when we were so aware of the presence of God that there had to be complete openness. There could be nothing kept hidden; everybody was transparent before everybody else and before God.

"This is the heart of revival: to be in the presence of God.

"We often use the term in revival: 'the Holy Spirit convicts people of sin.' What does this mean? What is conviction? Often we get a wrong picture in our minds, of the Holy Spirit pointing out our sins and saying 'Do something about it, or else . . .' Or we may imagine that it is like a child being caught redhanded doing something wrong, and the child cries.

"*How* does the Holy Spirit convict us of sin? It is *not* in that way, not like a child being caught. Rather, He brings us into the very presence of God so that we become aware of our sin, just like Isaiah who cried 'Woe is me! For I am lost; for I am a man of unclean lips . . .' (Isaiah 6:5) when he saw the Lord, the holy God, sitting upon a throne. It was because he was really in the presence of God that Isaiah realized what he was.

"We may think of it this way. Every home has a door, and whenever we go into a house, we enter through a door. We go through so many doors that it becomes just a habit. We enter without thinking much about it, whether we are going into a rich house or a poor one.

"Then imagine that you are going into a particular house, the home of a very wealthy man—the Prime Minister, perhaps. You walk straight into his house without thinking—and then suddenly you become aware of the beautiful carpet. The house is very 'posh.' You look at the purity of the beautiful carpet, and you think, 'Is there mud on my shoes?' Then you look down, and back—and yes, you have left muddy marks, and you think, 'What a mess!' It is a very real feeling, as you see the beautiful carpet spoiled by mud.

"Then you realize that the owner of the house is looking at you, and at the mud—and you feel that you want to clean the mud away with your tears, even, and that yet it would not be enough.

"It is like that with the very temple of God, your body. You see the dirty marks left inside His temple, and you want

**190**

to clean away those marks with your tears. But you do not have enough tears, and you know that no soap, no shampoo, can cleanse away those marks.

"But then it is as though you hear the words, 'No tears can wipe off those dirty marks; only the Blood of Jesus *can* cleanse you.'

"And you are glad and rejoice, and have a sense of indebtedness to God.

"That is how the Holy Spirit convicts of sin: by bringing us into the very presence of God, so that we compare ourselves with that holy Presence and become aware of our sinfulness. Then we are like Isaiah after he had cried, 'I am a man of unclean lips' when the angel took the piece of burning charcoal from the altar and said, ' . . . your guilt is taken away and your sin forgiven' (Isaiah 6:7).

"This is revival: when the Spirit of God brings us into His presence."

*Bishop Festo Kivengere*

# 22

# New
# Power and
# New
# Problems

When the Holy Spirit was poured out upon the Solomons, many found themselves in close touch with a God of power. To each, His power came in a different way.

As Jotham Ausuta said, "We saw bad men changed into good. I think of John Sitea, who was brought to court 75 times for robbery and even murder. By using the magic powers of evil spirits, he always managed to win his case. He was sent home to the Koio district, and there he came under conviction by the Holy Spirit. I prayed for his deliverance from the demons that were shaking and possessing him, and prayed for his cleansing by the blood of Christ.

"Then he was called back to court in Honiara because of previous trouble. When asked about it, he said, 'Yes. That was the old John.' He explained that he was the new John now, *Jesus'* John. But of course he was quite willing to bear the penalty for what the old John had done. The lawyer looked at him thoughtfully and said, 'Are you a Christian?' Then he looked at my son, Jeriel, Senior Inspector of Police, and said that John's case was acquitted. 'New John' is now a trusted member for the Koio district on the local governing council."

When Arnon Atomea was pastor of the two churches in Honiara, he made the comment: "There are many who spent a long time in 'the far country' away from God, who have now come back to Him. They have fully surrendered themselves to the Spirit, and have found reality. Longstanding bitterness between tribes has, in many cases, been melted away. In years past, deep-seated hatred, fears and blood-feuds left a barrier of enmity between people from different tribes: feelings which continued even between Christians. Now, however, they come together with tears in their eyes, and pray to God. On Malaita before, it was almost impossible for someone to forgive one who had committed adultery. The old custom was to seek revenge in some way; love and forgiveness seemed too hard even for Christians. Now, those who have already surrendered their hearts are able to forgive. We can see in this the wonder-working power of the Lord to change people, bringing the love of Christ into their lives."

One young woman, filled with joy in the Spirit, found herself facing adamant opposition from her husband. He forbade her to go to meetings, and hit her if she prayed. Once, he emptied the teapot over her. Sometimes her face was bruised and her nose would bleed, but her only reaction was perfect peace. Very much to her surprise, she didn't feel the slightest bitterness or anger towards her husband. Instead she found herself "strengthened with all power.... for all endurance and patience with joy" (Colossians 1:11). She continued to be a good wife and mother, and when her husband wanted to send her off to her parents' home, she refused to go. "I've married you," she said.

Even at that time, her husband said to her father, "I'm the one who's spoiling our home." Since then, he has come to know Christ in a new way, and is a changed man.

Another Malaita woman was troubled about her son who was far away from God. While he was home on holidays, she felt a compulsion to speak to him with concern at breakfast one morning.

"I began talking" she said, "and then the Holy Spirit took over. It wasn't me, although the words were spoken in my voice and I could hear them coming from my mouth. But it wasn't *me*—it was the Lord speaking through me to my son, telling him of things in his life that I knew nothing about. I simply had no idea of them." The boy admitted the truth of all that had been said about his life, and later that morning he put his complete trust in Jesus Christ. In time he went as a student to One Pusu for Bible training.

In the large church at Ambu one time, a woman stood up and said, "I was so blind that I couldn't walk along the track or I'd fall over anything that was in my way because I couldn't see it." She swung her hand around at all the 1500 people in the meeting, and said, "I want to tell you I can see you all here today! A miracle has happened to me."

Away in the Western Solomons, someone had put a "heathen curse" upon a woman and she had cried for three weeks. In desperation, she was brought to the S.S.E.C. team members, Cornelius and Shemuel. They prayed for her and immediately she was delivered.

The power of God was released in a new way among many people, but it met head-on the entrenched power of the Enemy.

In one village on Malaita, a promising young Christian had surreptitiously been using a "custom charm" or fetish of bark which was effective for healing purposes. His grandfather had given it to him. When revival came, the Spirit of God told him unmistakably that he must burn that piece of bark. Instead, he disobeyed and gave it away to his brother-in-law, telling him that it would help him as "medicine" against sickness.

Three days later, a terrible spirit of fear came upon him.

As he was walking along in the dark, it was as if this unseen thing came up to him, went down his throat and remained inside him. He was then under the power of this evil spirit, and often its voice spoke to him, threatening him with death in the very near future. He went once to a Christian meeting, and the spirit told him that if he went again, he would die. It also told him to stay inside all day and visit the burial ground at 2 a.m. Nobody else in the village knew about it, but he went there night after night.

More than once a team of Christians prayed for him, but he remained under that evil power for about a year, continually under threat of death.

At last, into his mind came the verse "My times are in Thy hands". He began to use that scriptural verse as a weapon against the evil spirit that kept threatening him. When the evil inner voice said "You'll die!" he would answer, "Scripture says, 'My times are in Thy hands,' so my times are in God's hands, not yours. It is God who has the right to decide when my time to die is to come, not you. And when I do die, I'll go to be with Him."

Gradually, as he kept fighting back with this verse from Scripture, the evil power over him began to weaken. In time, slowly, he became entirely freed from the grip it had upon him. His deliverance did not come with dramatic suddenness. It was a gradual process, but it was absolute.

As they faced such problems stirred up in the midst of revival, the S.S.E.C. leaders greatly appreciated a second visit by Bishop Festo Kivengere. It was during the revival which began in East Africa more than 40 years ago that Festo became a Christian. His experience of the movement of the Spirit within a young Church specially fitted him to give counsel and encouragement to the Church in the Solomons.

Festo gave wise advice on the importance of humility and brokenness as indispensable for the continuation of revival. He said, "May the Lord give you a spirit of openness and sensitivity to His promptings."

After his visit, Festo wrote, "The Lord has certainly revived His Church, and we praise His Name. So I am going back rejoicing. I am sure this is going to spread far and wide as the brethren learn to walk with Him."

Jeriel Gapu
Timothy Unaniasi

Jotham Ausuta
Ariel Bili

# 23

# A
# Fresh
# Outpouring

Summing up the revival in his homeland, an Islander wrote: "In the Solomons we have seen the outpouring of praise, joy, healing, love, wisdom, utterance, deliverance, visions, prophesy—and much more. And all these things are solely to glorify God in heaven. Though there has been error as well, God has given us the Holy Spirit of discernment to correct it."

The outpouring of the Spirit of God was not confined to one locality. Islanders were impelled to visit other districts and other islands with their message of new life. Some went to the Western Solomons, where 6000 men from Malaita worked in the plantations and logging camps. Others went as far afield as Papua New Guinea and the New Hebrides.

Fresh from such an experience of God's reviving power among their own people, a team of four Solomon Island pastors visited Papua New Guinea in mid-1972. In the S.S.E.M. Sepik field during their visit and for several months afterwards, many responded to the Spirit of God, testing a new reality, conviction and joy which they could not forget.

Then came a vicious counter-attack. In one church in particular, the power of evil gained an entrance, and there were some serious excesses. This brought about a fear of revival, but some people still continued to pray for renewal of the Church by the Holy Spirit. Three discouraging years went by, and the Christians felt despondent and powerless against the cults and darkness of sin. News of revival kept coming from the Solomons, but it seemed to have passed the Sepik people by.

Then in 1976, Barnabas Ke'in broke his arm, a seemingly irrelevant incident. He was General Superintendent of the newly-formed SSEC in the Sepik, but he found himself plucked out of his busy life and planted firmly in Wewak hospital to recover from a very complex fracture. During the weeks of convalescence and further illness, Barnabas became aware that God was speaking to him about his personal life, as well as the life of the Church, and what he should do about it. God showed him that it was he who stood in the way of revival.

Barnabas was visited by Jezreel Filoa, a Solomon Islander who had formerly been a missionary to the Sepik for many years. The two discussed Barnabas' concern, and cleared up the differences which had developed between them during the 1972 movement. Both men became convinced that God would soon do a mighty work, and Barnabas made up his mind to meet with the Ilahita elders to pray specifically for revival.

Ilahita is one of the biggest village clusters in New Guinea, with a population of some 1500. For countless years it has been the stronghold of the *tambaran* cult, a form of animist worship.

When Barnabas arrived there in June, he found that the elders and pastors of the whole Ilahita area were already waiting for him. The Holy Spirit had shown them, too, that God was about to send a revival. They had a sense of pressing urgency for their lives to be cleansed so that God could work unhindered, and they began immediately to confess their sins and make amends. At that stage, Barnabas was the only one able to counsel and pray with people because the other elders said, "We can't help anyone else yet. We have to set right so many things ourselves, first."

The Holy Spirit brought deep conviction of sin, and true sorrow and repentance. The men first put things right with each other, asking God's forgiveness; then they went to their wives and families to right wrongs, and even further afield, as necessary. When all was put right, to the best of their knowledge, they met together again in the church and began to praise God and pray for their fellow-Christians.

Outside, Christian villagers stopped to listen; there was something different about that singing in the church. "Do you hear that?" they said. "Revival has come!" Drawn by the sound of joy and life, they came streaming into the church, where the Spirit of God began to deal with each individual.

Meanwhile, into the church came some of the most important *tamberan* men and sorcerers who had scorned the Christian way for years. Almost against their wills, they found themselves drawn by a Power stronger than themselves and stronger than Satan who had so long enslaved them. They were brought under the influence of the almighty power of the living God who was at work in their hearts, bringing deep conviction of sin and evil so that they had to cry out and plead with God for mercy for their sins.

During this time and afterwards, many Christians were given dreams and visions. One, for example, saw a big water-tank with three faucets all choked with dirt and rust. Before the water could flow, those faucets had to be cleaned. Many, through similar dreams, were given assurance that after

God had cleansed His Church they would receive the Holy Spirit—the One who is like a river of living water flowing freely.

About that time, after many people's sins had been confessed and restitution made, Barnabas and some others were filled with the Holy Spirit and received gifts to minister to the people. This came about when they prayed and sang: suddenly they had great assurance and faith, and knew that they had received the Spirit. Certain gifts became evident: some had prophecy, some the power to preach, and some spoke in tongues. There were those who could discern hidden sins, and those who could identify people possessed by evil spirits, which would then be cast out in the name of Jesus. Some of the elders received gifts of wisdom and discernment to discern false words or teachings from true.

During that time, instead of much teaching or preaching, there was mostly individual counselling, open confession, singing, praying, exhorting, warning, instructing, prophesying and weeping. This went on for days, beginning at 5 a.m. and finishing at midnight or later. People would forget to eat; nobody felt hungry and nobody felt sleepy. They would sit there, watching, hungry for every word of God.

Confessions of sin were remarkably open because people did not try to hide anything. They were anxious to get rid of all wrongdoing, and they called each detail by its name, mentioning times, persons involved or amounts as completely as possible. Sorcerers and men who had been deeply involved in *tamberan* activities confessed their trickery, suppression of the truth, multiple murders and all the evils that go with sorcery and idolatry. They simply wanted to wipe the slate clean.

When the Holy Spirit put His finger on something else that grieved Him, the one convicted would immediately return to an elder and frankly confess the sin. He would apologize to his wife then, perhaps, or tell someone he was sorry for having argued violently about land or pigs. Where possible, he would make amends for his wrongdoing; each day, many stolen plates, spoons and pens were returned to their rightful owners. Those who had put their trust in charms and fetishes brought them along to be viewed, burned and thrown away.

One striking feature of this present movement has been the emphasis on unity among the leadership, in contrast to the 1972 movement. Whenever something has threatened to creep in and disrupt that unity, the leaders have stopped everything to pray and confess one to another, until full unity and love has been restored.

As Peter Jost made clear in his account, "The key word in this movement is *brokenness....* The Lord wants broken people and nothing else. Without brokenness, there can be none of His working, no blessing, no Spirit released. Often someone will pray like this: 'Lord, I have a heart of stone. I've been concerned about myself, and not about the salvation of the lost ones. *I* want to be someone; *I* want a name; *I* want honor. I'm concerned about myself and not about You. Please break me, grind me to dust, so that there is nothing left but You.'"

At first, the movement did not spread rapidly from Ilahita to other areas. Though leaders elsewhere felt the need for renewal, many churches wanted God's blessings but shunned the sacrificial cost. Most of them wanted a shortcut, and it soon became evident that nobody could force the Spirit of the Lord. Though He Himself was ready, unless there was unity, willingness to repent, and a brokenness amongst the church leaders, He was hindered from working.

After the annual SSEC conference in August, however, news came from Dieter Volz. "We had a good conference," he wrote. "Business was several times delayed just because the Lord worked so deeply in the hearts of people that meetings were simply stopped for prayer and ministry. The Spirit of God also moved amongst missionaries, and after a time of open confession of things held against each other (for years, in some cases) we felt drawn much closer to each other.

This led to clear confession and apologies on the part of missionaries toward New Guineans, who responded in the same way.

"Church leaders from different areas were touched by the Spirit of God and returned home with great joy." Dieter added, "We can say that the revival is spreading into other areas. . . . Much prayer for a deepening and consolidating work of the Spirit is needed now.

*Michael Maeliau*

# 24

# "Let
# Us
# Draw
# Near"

Early in 1975, on his way home to the Solomons after three years at the Bible College of New Zealand, Michael Maeliau was speaking to a gathering in Sydney. It was more than 80 years since his countryman, Peter Ambuofa, had begun to share with his people the Good News. Now here was Michael sharing in Australia the insights which the Holy Spirit of God had given him.

"Prayer is the highest and purest form of ministry," he began. "There is a sense in which we are in the presence of God at all times, but there is a real sense in which we make a definite act of entering His presence. It may be in a group, but more often in private.

"In Old Testament times, the High Priest had the privilege of entering the Sanctuary once a year only. Often people in these days make the mistake of thinking, 'Christ died and the veil of the temple was rent, so that means that we are all in the Sanctuary all the time.'

"This is not so. The Holiest of Holies is *not* made a common place. The rending of the veil had a different significance. First, it showed that the earthly tabernacle (the Temple and all associated with it) was no longer needed. The real had come, so the time for all that foreshadowed it was past. Secondly, the veil was rent to show that *anyone* could go in at any time, not just the High Priest on one occasion in the year.

"We read in Hebrews 4:16 that there is a definite *act* of entering into the Sanctuary, into the presence of God: 'Let us then with boldness draw near to the throne of grace, that we may receive mercy and find grace to help in time of need.'

"Too often we are presumptuous; we rush into prayer, thinking that we are already in the Sanctuary. But we are told to *enter* into God's holy presence.

"How can we enter? 'By the blood of Jesus, by the new and living way,' as we read in Hebrews 10:19-22: 'Therefore, brethren, since we have boldness to enter the sanctuary by the blood of Jesus, by the new and living way which he opened for us through the curtain, that is, through his flesh, and since we have a great priest over the house of God, let us draw near with a true heart in full assurance of faith, with our hearts sprinkled clean from an evil conscience and our bodies washed with pure water.'

"We make a definite time when we say, 'Let me draw near', like the High Priest of old, by faith, through the Blood.

"During any revival, there always comes a new emphasis on the Blood of Christ. People think once more of the power of the Blood, of protection by the Blood.

"Often it is thought that the Blood is just picture-language, but the lifeblood of Jesus is a real thing, not the blood of a phantom. It is real blood. We do not think of it as the Roman Catholics do, objectifying it in the wine of communion. But, like the High Priest of Old Testament times, we could not enter into the Holiest of Holies, were it not for the Blood. The Blood is something we can claim and lay hold of by faith.

"In practice, this means two things: first, the confession of sins. We cannot presume that 'I'm fine. I'll go right now into God's presence.' Into the Holiest of Holies, we must enter by the Blood; we cannot enter presumptuously.

"Second, what does the Blood stand for? It is our only plea. We are not worthy on our own merit. We say to God, 'This is the only ground on which I can come to You: the Blood of Jesus.'

"This Sanctuary, the Holiest of Holies, is where we should offer our prayers. As we see in the Old Testament (Exodus 25:22) it is on the Mercy Seat that God has promised to meet us. That is where *communion* with God takes place.

"This requires a definite act. It is really in the Sanctuary that we should make intercession. We are like Abraham speaking to God concerning Sodom and Gomorrah (Genesis 18:16-33): we remember that we are but 'dust and ashes' and yet we can speak to God face to face.

"In Hebrews 9:24 we read: 'For Christ has entered, not into a sanctuary made with hands, a copy of the true one, but into heaven itself, now to appear in the presence of God on our behalf'. This, the Holiest of Holies, is where Christ is interceding for us. The Priest (He is our High Priest) must appear there to plead, and we too.

"Many times we are ignorant that all our prayers are made outside the Sanctuary and that they are mere communication, like a person-to-person long-distance phone call. God needs more than communication from us. He needs more than face-to-face conversation with us. What He longs for is heart-to-heart *communion* with us—and *that* is the heart of personal revival, when our prayers can be effective.

"The place, the Holiest of Holies, is open—but do not treat it as a common place. Do not presume that you are already in. Make a definite act: 'draw near.'

"Without the Blood, you cannot enter the Sanctuary, into the presence of God—neither in the Old Testament nor in the New. We may enter into that most holy place on the sole ground of Christ's death."

With clean hearts, let us see the Door. It is open. Let us enter it with boldness. The King of Glory is within; let us bow in adoration. Let us worship Him. Let us ask Him to sprinkle our hearts deeply and inwardly with His most precious Blood. Let Him anoint us for all service in His Name. Let Him continually pour forth His Spirit upon us so that His joy and power may remain with us. In our day-to-day lives, let us remain there seated "together with Him in the heavenly places." He longs to do these things for us.

"What things soever ye desire, when ye pray, believe that ye receive them, and ye shall have them."